With the Peasants of Aragón

With the Peasants of Aragón

Libertarian Communism in the Liberated Areas

Augustin Souchy Bauer

with an additional chapter by
Victor Blanco

THEORY AND PRACTICE

'Entre los Campesinos de Aragón: el Comunismo Libertario en las Comarcas Liberadas'

First published 1937, *Tierra y Libertad*, Barcelona

First English edition published 1982
In Europe by Cienfuegos Press
In the USA by Soil of Liberty

This edition
2017 Theory and Practice

www.theoryandpractice.org.uk

ISBN: 978-0-9956609-0-8

Translated from the original Spanish by Abe Bluestein

Contents

Introduction

I first met Augustin Souchy in the Casa CNT-FAI (Headquarters of the National Confederation of Labour [CNT] and the Iberian Anarchist Federation [FAI]), Barcelona, April 30, 1937. He was the head of Information in Foreign Languages for the CNT-FAI. He greeted me like an old friend and told me I was to start working as the English Language correspondent for the CNT-FAI the following Monday, May 3rd.

We had never met before, yet I felt I knew him from his reputation. He was waiting for me to arrive to fill a vacancy on the basis of a letter of introduction from Mark Mratchny, editor of the *Freie Arbeiter Stimme, 'Free Voice of Labour'*, the Yiddish Anarchist weekly in New York City.

When I was there about two months, Souchy arranged a trip through Aragón for my wife, Selma and me. It would cover some of the ground that he travelled and about which he was writing a book. Although I remained in Spain until January 1938, I did not see Souchy's book at that time.

We saw part of Aragón, the towns and villages that Souchy reports about in his book, *With The Peasants of Aragón*. We did not see the FAI concentration camp for fascist prisoners and captured prisoners of war that Souchy describes, where the guards sleep, eat and work with the prisoners and are indistinguishable from the prisoners. But we did see a group of 40 or 50 prisoners of war in a village on a mountain top about 50 yards behind the front line trenches. They were working on the road and there was not a single guard anywhere in sight.

I asked who was guarding the prisoners and the guide answered with a shrug of his shoulders: 'No one.' He explained that the prisoners were draftees in Franco's army, from poor homes. They were living better than ever before in their lives, and living safe from the dangers of war. They shared the homes of the villagers, ate with the villagers, and were doing the same kind of work as the people of the village.

No prisoner had ever tried to escape. None had ever tried to seize a gun.

I knew that I was seeing something new in the history of warfare on a small scale. I did not dream that comrade Souchy had seen and written about a large camp for fascists and war prisoners, also run on similar libertarian principles.

Selma and I saw about two dozen towns and villages on that trip. We saw the collectives, the consumers' cooperatives set up in former churches, stores and shops owned by individual shopkeepers. We observed that we did not see a single policeman or armed guard in any of the communities, including those right on the front lines.

At that time, we did not know that there were no police or armed security forces in a large area embracing several hundred towns and villages with a population of half a million people living on the front lines and in the war zones of a most bitterly fought struggle.

Souchy's report of his trip through Aragón is a product of first hand observation and lifelong dedication to the deepest principles of libertarian communism. He was part of the mainstream during the Civil War when 8,000,000 people out of 12,000,000 in the loyalist half of Spain worked and/or lived in industrial or agricultural collectives.

A Few Words About The Author:

Although he is well known in Europe, he is not so well known in the English-speaking world. Augustin Souchy Bauer was born August 28, 1892 [died, Munich 1984]. In 1917, he escaped from Germany to avoid the draft. He then was expelled from Sweden to Norway and from Norway to Denmark because of his participation in anti-war activities.

In 1918, he started writing articles and books for the anarchist and anarcho-syndicalist movement, and continues to lecture and write actively to this day, at 89 years of age.

He has had a knack to be at the centre of historic developments during his life that few, if any, could equal. He was in Russia in 1920 for eight months in connection with the first International Congress of Red Trade Unions.

He lived in Germany from 1921 to 1933 when Hitler came to power. He served as editor of *Der Syndicalist*, organ of the German anarcho syndicalist labour organization. He was a founder of the International Working Men's Association, IWMA, the anarcho-syndicalist international, and was co-secretary of the International with Rudolf Rocker and Alexander Shapiro.

After 1931 when it became a Republic, he went to Spain many times as a representative of the IWMA. He was in Spain in 1936, two weeks before the outbreak of the Spanish Civil War and Social Revolution. He was immediately put in charge of information in foreign countries and was an adviser on foreign relations.

In 1939, fleeing ahead of Franco's troops, Souchy left Barcelona with half-a-million Spanish anti-fascists. Since then, Souchy has spent a great deal of time in Mexico. He visited Israel and wrote about their collective settlements. He travelled through most of South America, and has spent time in Africa teaching trade union organisation to the native populations. He has lectured and written in Sweden, Germany, the United States, and in many other countries. His books and articles have been published in German, French, English, Swedish, Danish, Spanish and Yiddish.

At age 89, he still conducts active campaigns in behalf of anarchism and anarcho-syndicalism with lectures and writing in Germany as well as recent visits to Sweden and Israel.

***

The social and economic story of Aragón was the finest chapter of that period. A majority of the 500,000 people in that rural area put their personal property into the collectives voluntarily and committed their families to the free and equal life of libertarian communism. But individualists lived among them and enjoyed the respect of their neighbours.

The voluntary character of the social transformation from private ownership to collective communities is described at length in the first person account of what happened in the town of Alcampel. (*See addendum.*) About half of the town goes collective. Among those who do not join are three teamsters who drive their own trucks, the only trucks in the town. The Collective cannot function without some means of transportation. Does the Collective requisition the trucks? No. They understand and respect the fear of the teamsters; they could lose their livelihood if they gave up their trucks. So, the Collective leaves the only three trucks in town in private hands and sends a delegation to Barcelona to obtain a truck.

How did it happen that the spirit of liberty had such strong roots in Spain, that 8,000,000 of 12,000,000 people lived or worked in voluntary collectives in Loyalist Spain, without benefit of government decrees requiring compliance with regulations from above?

The libertarian labour movement was born in Spain in October 1868, following a visit by Giuseppe Fanelli, an Italian comrade and supporter of Michael Bakunin in the fight within the First International Workingmen's Association between the authoritarian Karl Marx and the anarchist Bakunin.

A great ferment of opposition to the existing reactionary monarchist regime in Spain was developing. Labour unions were fighting for the right to exist in the cities. In the countryside, landless day labourers and small tenant farmers dreamed of an end to hunger and deprivation, and fought for the right to earn a living on the land. They fought for a new social order without exploitation and oppression. The different nationality regions of Spain were calling for greater autonomy, for federalism.

The message of the Libertarian wing of the First International was: the liberation of the working class is the task of the workers themselves; direct action; federalism; libertarian communism as the goal of social transformation.

The libertarian movement was about 70 years old at the time of the Civil War. Its history was a history of struggle and sacrifice from the very beginning. Its message was heard all over the country, by the starving agricultural labourers and petty tenant farmers in the rural areas, and by the oppressed, underpaid industrial workers in the cities. Anarchist unions grew strong in the country and the cities. There were long periods of oppression and persecution, and short periods of relative freedom when they were even able to publish dally papers.

In 1910, the separate unions organised the National Confederation of Labour (CNT) at a founding congress in Barcelona. It was different from all other national labour organisations and parties. It was – and is to this day – a decentralised organization, with maximum autonomy in the local unions and local central labour councils. It never set up leaders who spoke for the entire organisation, or central executive bodies that could make decisions for the whole movement.

Decisions started in the local union, went through delegates to city or district Labour Councils, and finally to the National Plenum of Regions and the National Secretariat. CNT unions never confined themselves to bread and butter issues. Spain was a closed society, ruled by Church and Army for the benefit of a wealthy few. The overwhelming majority were always hungry, ill housed, poorly clothed and illiterate. Freedom of speech and all of the civil liberties taken for granted in the United States and the western democracies did not exist in Spain except for short periods of freedom after long years of dictatorship and oppression.

The CNT was always in the vanguard of the struggle for freedom. Its history is filled with martyrs who gave their lives fighting oppression. The movement put great stress on libertarian and rational education for children and adults. And it always kept the goal of libertarian communism high in its order of priorities.

When the army and the fascists rose against the Republic on July 19 1936, their most vigorous opposition was the labour movement in the big cities, in whose front ranks were the Anarchists and the CNT. They overcame the armed forces and the fascists in the cities. Owners and executives of big business fled with the army. Wealthy landowners abandoned their lands. The workers and their unions lost no time taking control of the factories and the farms, the railroads, utilities, municipal services, the schools, hospitals, bakeries and dairies. Everything was collectivised. The workers through their unions and factory councils ran everything.

In the country the peasants, together with almost everyone else in the towns and villages – bakers and butchers, construction workers and dressmakers, doctors and teachers and lawyers, met in open assemblies and freely voted to organise collectives and enter into a new way of life. Those who wanted to work and live alone in privately owned shops were permitted to do so without interference and with one simple limitation: they could not hire anyone to work for them.

The collectives in Aragón probably reached the highest level of libertarian communism in Spain during the Civil War, 1936-1939.

The original book was published by *Tierra y Libertad* (Land and Liberty) in Barcelona, in 1937. The new volume adds a first person account of what happened in one village, Alcampel, as an appendix to Souchy's report. *With The Peasants of Aragón* is a vital chapter of the Spanish Civil War and Social Revolution.

Abe Bluestein – 1981

Foreword

The following report was published in 1937 in Spanish and Swedish, and later in German. Today (1981) the number of people who were alive at the time of the Spanish Civil War is relatively small. A short introduction may be helpful for the younger generation.

The Civil War began in July 1936, when Franco started his military action with the help of Mussolini and Hitler. It was a typical Spanish '*pronunciamento*' against the Spanish Republic.

Thanks to the extraordinary and heroic struggle of the Spanish people, and in particular the anarcho-syndicalist movement which advocated direct action continuously starting in the 19th century, the Franco 'putsch' was defeated in one half of the country during the first week.

However, the struggle degenerated into a long civil war in which Franco finally emerged victorious because the Republic was abandoned by the democratic western world.

The most characteristic feature of that historic chapter, however, was not the military struggle but the construction of a new economy, a new society by manual and professional workers without the interference of politicians or government. While the Russian Revolution of 1917-1918 was the realisation of the theory of Karl Marx, the Spanish Social Revolution was carried out in the spirit and thought of Proudhon, Bakunin and Kropotkin.

I was in Barcelona when the Civil War broke out. As soon as the collectivisation of industry and agriculture began, I decided to dedicate myself to the study of it. I knew that collectivisation was not a gift from heaven but the result of action by working people. The goal of the Spanish anarcho-syndicalists from their very beginning was to take over the economy and organise it on a collectivised basis.

Several attempts were made after the proclamation of the Republic in 1931 to take over private enterprise and convert to a collectivised system, but they did not last because State power and the police dissolved them quickly. However, when the military forces were crushed in 1936 and public power was in the hands of the Revolution – the Chief of Police in Barcelona was the well-known anarchist Eroles – there was no power to prevent the realisation of the old dream to build a new free society based on social equality and justice. I wanted to make a record of these new developments and preserve them for the future.

Collectivisation in Spain was the most important transformation in history, both of the property structure of the land and the means of production, and the organization of productive work. The collectives were a realisation of the ideals and theories of free or libertarian socialism, in contrast with the Russian state kolkhoz and even the self-management system in Yugoslavia. I saw this as I travelled through these countries to study their systems. The Spanish farm collectives were most similar to the Moshov Shitufi, one of the various types of working communities known as *kibbutzim* in Israel.

The Spanish Communist Party opposed the collectives during the Civil War. After the war Franco destroyed them. I revisited Spain thirty years later to acquaint myself with the political, economic and social situation. The technological progress that had developed throughout the world after the Second World War had also reached Spain. German, French, British and American multi-national companies have their subsidiaries in Spain. Like the dictator Peron in Argentina, Franco had introduced social security and unemployment insurance. Illiteracy had dropped from 50% to 15%. Conveniences of modern living such as radios, televisions, refrigerators and automobiles are no longer the privilege of a small minority.

There was also a change in the countryside. Before the Civil War, Spain was half agricultural, half industrial. Now only 30% of the population depends on agriculture. In some parts of the country the peasants have improved their economic situation through mutual aid. Partly as a result of memories of the collectives, partly because of general progress, cooperatives, which did not exist before, have been organised to improve methods of work, transportation, and buying and selling. According to an official report there are now 15,000 cooperatives of small farmers in Spain. It is reported that in the Province of Cuenca 14,000 farmers with less than 37 acres each have decided to organise cooperatives. These figures may not be accurate, but it cannot be denied that there is a cooperative movement among the farmers.

There is still a social abyss, especially in Andalusia, between the big landowners, or '*latifundistas*', and the poor peasants. However, the political climate is not revolutionary at the present time.

The transition from the military dictatorship to the

constitutional monarchy was peaceful. During several visits to Spain since the death of Franco, I tried to find out if the workers and peasants are ready to fight now for a new libertarian, or at least democratic republic. The majority of the answers were negative. There is no push for violent revolution at this time among the Spanish people. And the adherents and partisans in the army of a new military dictatorship are such a small minority that they cannot risk trying to make another counterrevolution. The Civil War from 1936 to 1939 cost the lives of 1,000,000 victims. The Spanish people do not want a repetition of that experience. There is one question a Spanish comrade asked me during one of my recent visits to Spain: Do you think that the collectivisation that was carried out during the Civil War can be repeated in the near future? My answer: History never repeats itself in the same way or the same form. The same revolution cannot be made twice.

This does not mean, however, that the struggle for a collective or cooperative economy, based upon the common ownership of the land and the means of production, is obsolete. These are still the goals today and for the future. But the starting point is different today than 1936. The technical and industrial evolution since then will impress their mark on social change.

At this time Spain finds itself in a period of transition politically. The workers are engaged in hard struggles for economic demands. The country is torn with bitter conflicts for regional autonomy by national minorities. If after several years the current struggles are resolved and the present State authority is still in power, new political and social problems will surface. As long as the libertarian traditions and the spirit of renewal remain vibrant in the

Spanish Labour Movement the goals for the realisation of the perennial human ideals will live: Liberty, Equality, Fraternity.

Augustin Souchy

A New Way of Life is Born in Aragón

Battles between peasants and fascists broke out in towns and villages throughout Aragón immediately after July 19 1936. In many of the villages the peasants fled to escape the persecution of the fascists. Later, when the antifascist columns entered Aragón from Catalonia and the Levant, the towns and villages were liberated from the Civil Guards and fascists. The peasants returned to their homes. A social transformation then took place that was not equalled anywhere else in Spain for its depth and organisation.

Unlike Catalonia, distribution of land in Aragón did not make for very great extremes of wealth and poverty. The majority of the people were small farmers, tenant farmers and sharecroppers. Sharecroppers worked for the few large landholders, as did the landless day labourers. (Both these groups had to find work in the cities for many months of the year because Mother Earth could not feed them.) The war tended to eliminate even these extremes rather quickly, for, as the popular militia advanced, the large landholders and the fascists fled the region. Very few remained to work with the peasants.

The people of the villages held general town meetings in the public plazas and agreed to expropriate the lands of the fascist landholders. Other land was also collectivised or turned over to the village. The people agreed to work together in collectives in almost all the liberated communities. Five hundred towns and villages with a population of approximately half-a-million people established collectivism, a type of economy and social system unknown in modern Europe until then. The transformation of private property into a system of collective property was accomplished in a relatively short time and to a surprising degree.

Collectivisation in Aragón constituted a final stage in the transformation of rural life that had been fought for since the start of the Republic in 1931. The agrarian reform offered by the Republic provided no help for the rural proletariat. Very few large landholders were expropriated under the banner of reform. Only the lands belonging to the Church or religious orders were taken over. These were distributed among a relatively small number of peasant families, but the rural masses continued to live in misery.

When the power of reaction was destroyed after July 19 1936, the peasants realised their ideal: collectivisation. Communes also took control of the land in all the towns and villages of Loyalist Spain. But the process of collectivisation did not develop as far anywhere else in Spain as it did in Aragón.

Collectivisation was not ordered by the State or imposed by force as in Russia. The great majority of the peasants supported the ideals of the social revolution. Their goal was to produce collectively and to distribute the product of their labour with justice to all. No one issued a proclamation for a particular type of collectivisation. There were no decrees, no government commissions to issue orders, no official orientation to direct the peasants. They acted according to their intuitions. An active minority led the way. The ideal of libertarian communism was strong among the peasants. It was stirring to see how the peasants could hit the nail on the head with their clear, humane thinking even though they did not have a great deal of theory or deep knowledge. With the intuition that people have in exceptional times, the rural population went to work to construct a new life.

News of the collectivisation and libertarian communism in Aragón spread throughout the country. But the actual content of collectivist life in Aragón was not known elsewhere in Spain or abroad. A description of how they were organised, how they reached understandings, had not yet been written. The story of the social revolution in Aragón after July 19th was not yet told.

However, what took place in Aragón is of greatest importance to the world socialist movement. More than half-a-million peasants, impelled by necessity, by their misery and their ideals, took destiny into their own hands. Equality, Liberty, Fraternity, the great dreams of the French Revolution, have not yet been realised in the world. They were being realised in Aragón. The peasant was free from political oppression and the exploitation of the great landholders. Liberty was won in battle. Equality was organised. Fraternity lived in the hearts of the people..

Structure of the Collectives in Aragón

The smallest unit of the collective in Aragón was the work group, usually numbering five to ten members, sometimes more. The group might consist of friends, or the neighbours on a certain street, or a group of small farmers, tenant farmers, or day labourers. When one group finished its work, it would help another group. Everyone was obliged to work. Each group member was given a workers' card. A group would go out to work together led by their delegate, who much of the time worked with his comrades as well as recording the members' work; the collective assigned land to the groups. The tools, machinery, and animals needed for work were the property of the collective. The cultivation of the land assigned to them was the responsibility of the group.

The collective was the free community of labour of the villagers. It was created with the influence of anarchist ideas. The CNT and the FAI (National Confederation of Labour and Iberian Anarchist Federation) held general assemblies in all the villages. Peasants, small farmers and tenant farmers attended. That was how the collectives were born. They took possession of the land and the tools and machinery of the expropriated landholders. The small farmers and tenant farmers who joined the collective brought their tools and equipment. An inventory of all property and equipment was made. Whoever did not wish to join the collective could keep the land that he could cultivate without hired labour. Each collective proceeded along the following lines of development:

The distribution of land, labour, tools and fruit of their toil was taken care of first. The collective has to be concerned in the first place with the material survival of its members. The product of the fields was brought to a common warehouse; the most important foods were distributed equally among all. Surplus crops were used for trade with other communes or with collectives in the cities. Produce was distributed to the members free of charge. Depending on the wealth of the commune there would be bread and wine. Sometimes bread, meat and other foods were issued without limit and free of charge. Whatever had to be acquired outside of the commune, through barter or purchase from other communes or the cities, or commodities that were in low supply in the commune, were rationed. Everyone, whether able to work or not, received the necessities of life as far as the collective could provide them. The underlying idea was no longer 'a good day's pay for a good day's work', but 'from each according to their ability, to each according to their needs'.

Herein lay one difference between the peasant collectives in Aragón and the industrial and commercial collectives in Catalonia and other parts of Spain. In industry, labour or production was collectivised. Consumption remained individual. In the peasant collectives consumption as well as production was collectivised. The new system was simple in its basic characteristics, varied in forms of application. The customary compensation was quotas and rationing for things that were scarce, unlimited distribution of goods that were in abundance. These are the economic forms of libertarian communism.

The District Federation embraced all the local collectives in the district. Ten to twenty communes joined together to form an economic unit. The labour collective in each village sent an exact inventory to the Regional Federation reporting the amount of land, machines, means of transport, harvest, property and merchandise on hand. The District Federation maintained warehouses and marketed the agricultural produce of all the affiliated villages and collectives; products for interchange were sent to the Regional Federation and in some cases to Barcelona. The collectives were able to obtain the goods they needed with the credit built up by the produce they sent to the District. The majority of the District Federations had ample warehouse facilities. The villages were able to obtain what they needed. Everything they needed could be found in the District.

The District Federation was composed of delegates elected by the collectives of the villages. They were responsible for communication and transportation between the villages; they bought new means of transportation, installed additional telephone lines and supported cultural progress in the affiliated villages. The District Federations led the defence against reactionaries and fascists during the first months after July 19th. Local Defence Councils received arms and strategic advice from the District Federation. The District Federation in the Barbastro Zone, Huesca Province, conducted the defence against fascism for nine months. They provided food and all necessary war materials to the militia.

All the District Federations of Aragón belonged to

the Aragón Regional Federation of Collectives. The Committee of this Regional Federation was the economic centre of the entire region. During the first months there was a certain amount of duplication. The Aragón Defence Council assumed responsibility for defence at the beginning. The Defence Council was recognised by the Government as the official representative body of the region. It had the characteristics of a governmental body. Actually, there was no Defence Council, only an Economic Council.

A Congress of District Federations was held in Caspe in February 1937. They agreed to make the Regional Federation the economic centre of the agricultural collectives of Aragón. The District Federations would send their produce or other goods to the Regional Federation. The interchange of goods between sections of Aragón could be done through the Regional federation. Where necessary, there would be transactions with other regions or other countries.

This, briefly, was the structure of the collectives of Aragón. Following is our report of what we saw in some of the villages, the District Federations and the Regional Federation on how the new economy functioned on a foundation of equality and justice.

Collectivism was not new in Spain. Nor was it limited to Aragón. However, it was most widespread in Aragón. The CNT and the anarchists were the most fervent supporters of collectivisation, but not the only ones. The members of the UGT (General Union of Workers – Socialist) also favoured collectivisation in the city and the country. Spanish anarcho-syndicalism was the main spark and inspiration of the idea and the movement. The socialist and syndicalist unions worked together frequently, with equal zeal for collectivisation in the rural areas. Collectivisation spread steadily in the villages and towns of the region.

A Congress of all the unions of Aragón was held in Caspe, February 22, 1937. It was called by the CNT, but the UGT in Aragón also participated. The spirit of this great movement crystallised at the Congress. The resolution expressing this follows:

> Understanding that the program of the two signatory organisations cannot be realised for the moment, particularly if we take into account the diversity of programs of the different sectors of the antifascist front, and recognising that any attempt to implant a particular type of economic and political system would be suicidal and fatal for the struggle we support, the CNT and the UGT accept the following bases for unity of action:
>
> 1) We undertake to fulfil all the orders of the legitimate government of the Spanish Republic and the Council of Aragón in which our respective organisations are represented, using all our influence and resources for this purpose.
>
> 2) A Regional Coordinating Commission will be established within eight days after this agreement has been signed; it will promote unity of action, resolve conflicts that may arise between the two organisations in view of the lamentable divisions between us until now and eliminate elements who may have infiltrated into

our organisations.

The Coordinating Commission will establish its internal organization with comrades of both organisations from the three provinces to facilitate the resolution of conflicts.

The Regional Coordinating Commission will determine with which of the two union federations new unions shall affiliate according to the facts presented.

We reject all force to compel an individual to belong to one or the other union.

The Aragón provincial secretaries of the Spanish Federation of Agricultural Workers of the UGT undertake the study of the structure of the Regional Federation of Collectives of the CNT as quickly as possible in accordance with resolutions adopted by their Congress to create a single organization to strengthen agriculture in Aragón.

The Regional Confederation of Labour (CNT) and the General Union of Workers (UGT) state that the seizure of properties of fascist elements be declared legal, whether they be in agriculture, in the cities or in industry, and that the properties shall be transferred to Municipal Councils which will place them at the disposition of labour organisations to be collectivised. Both organisations support the disposition of such properties made by the Council of Aragón.

Both organisations will respect decisions reached freely by the peasants to administer themselves as they wish and the unions can campaign for the spread of collectivisation pointing out the advantages of this form of organization. The CNT and the UGT will assist and stimulate freely organised collectives which can serve as examples for other workers and peasants

This was the pact of the two organisations. The UGT was on record in favour of collectivisation. The pact was limited to Aragón only. The national organisations of the CNT and the UGT did not reach an agreement on collectivisation of the land throughout Spain. The CNT wanted socialisation through collectivisation; the UGT preferred nationalisation. This was to be limited to large properties. The large landed estates would be expropriated and transferred to the State. Production and consumption in the villages were not changed, and continued with its capitalist disorder. Small private property and individual cultivation of the land was not changed.

The Socialist and the Communist Party also failed to support collectivisation. The agrarian program of both parties followed the agrarian reform of the Republic. None of their proposals went beyond the official agrarian reform program, which was limited to the distribution of the large landed estates. Agricultural workers must be made small property owners. France did this during the Great Revolution. Result: a nation of small farmers, a social class that bears the seed of capitalism and conservatism.

The Communist Party advocated the creation of agricultural cooperatives instead of a program of collectivisation. They published a set of model by-laws for such agricultural cooperatives in their publication, l*a Voz del Campo* (Voice of the Country), May 22, 1937, Valencia. They did not speak of collectivisation. They based their proposal for cooperatives on private property. This was in contrast with the program of forced collectivisation of the peasants in Russia, an ambiguous position for the Communist International.

Cooperatives could satisfy Spain's peasants as little as the government's program of agrarian reform. Both kept private property as the basis for farming. Agricultural workers went beyond such petty-bourgeois reforms after July 19th, without waiting for the political parties. They were inspired with the ideal of communism, filled with a deep desire for liberty. They wanted nothing of the private economy of capitalism. They wanted to work together collectively and distribute the product of their labour to all justly. They believed that they could achieve this goal with collectives. They went beyond all halfway solutions, all superficial reforms. Collectivism was the principle of libertarian communism. The individual peasant clinging stubbornly to his piece of private property was not their ideal. The collective was the centrepiece for the birth of the new society. It triumphed over individualism. Collectivism was to be the cradle for the rebirth of Spain.

[Souchy's description of the new society developing in the towns and villages of Aragón was written in the present tense as a report of what was taking place in '37. To appreciate the dramatic impact of his book when it was published while the Civil War was still going on, I have retained his report as he wrote it in the present tense. *Translator A.B.*]

Alcañiz

An attractive town of 8,000 people close to the provincial capital, Caspe. There were few fascists in Alcañiz, and there was no fighting. Immediately after July 19th, the workers agreed on expropriation of the property of the fascists and collectivisation of the land. The CNT and the FAI were in the majority. There was no resistance to collectivisation. The UGT, very weak at the beginning, grew stronger in the following months. The CNT did not accept members who rejected collectivisation, so the individualists joined the UGT. UGT membership reached 1,600. The CNT had 1,700 members. In addition, there were four FAI groups and approximately 300 members in the Libertarian Youth (FIJL). The newspaper in the town is called *Cultura y Accion* (Culture and Action), published twice a week. Its editor, a militant of the Libertarian Youth, is Manuel Salas.

Stores are not collectivised. Small merchants continue to operate their stores as in the past. Transportation is collectivised. Housing is the property of the municipality. There is no charge for electricity or water. The town has two movie houses. They are collectivised by the UGT and the CNT. The majority of the workers, 32, belong to the CNT, 5 to the UGT.

The priests fled. The church was not burned. It

serves as a warehouse for the collective. The different sections are marked on the church's pillars: shoes and sandals here; soap and other cleaning materials; meats and sausage; preserves and other provisions; fabrics and cloth. Potatoes are stored near the main altar. Noodles and spaghetti are made in another part of the church. Offices have been set up. Nothing can be obtained with money, only with vouchers. Each member of the collective has a membership card and a book of vouchers. People are given what they request and it is recorded in the book of vouchers. The public enters through the main front door. The side doors are used for delivery of supplies. The church is the local market place.

The CNT has six seats on the Municipal Council, the UGT an equal number. The president is a CNT member. They work a nine-hour day while the war against fascism continues. Wages are not abolished completely. A member receives ten pesetas for a day's work. Bread is 0.60 pesetas a kilo; meat, 4.50; potatoes, 0.65; olive oil, 2.10; wine, 0.90; sugar, 1.80.

The collective has new presses to extract oil from olives, three flour mills and an electrical generator powered by waterfalls. Since the collective was formed, all the children can go to school. The teachers belong to the UGT.

There are 500 agricultural workers in the collective as producers and consumers, one large family. They do not work for wages in the traditional sense. The members of the collective work on farms that previously belonged to fascists. One of them produces 36,000 kilos of olive oil per year, besides wine, wheat and oats. The farm has six horses but not one cow. The second collective belonged to the marquis. No dairy cows there either. There was a shortage of milk in a majority of the villages. No milk was given to the children, only to the sick. A majority of the collective's members live in the town, although they work in the fields. Every Sunday they are given a free meal in the collective cafe plus five pesetas for their 'petty vices,' such as tobacco, etc.

The collective is not doing very well yet. For the 150 families they need 1,450 kilos of bread a week (300 grams per person daily), 100 grams of meat, a litre of wine daily, half a kilo of sugar per week and 1.5 kilos of chocolate.

For several months they did not have a single dairy cow. In June 1937, they bought five cows and built a barn for them. They obtained cloth from a collective in the city in exchange for some of their produce. Tobacco is provided free at times, but rarely.

The collective is not wealthy, but its members are happy. Everyone has little, but they know that equality and justice prevails, and this knowledge gives them the enthusiasm and the moral strength to build their new community.

A FAI Concentration Camp

There is a concentration camp at Valmuel, in Alcañiz Township, Teruel Province. The country is a desert without a single tree for many kilometres around. A number of buildings have been erected at the foot of a hill. Dormitories, inspection rooms, stables... everything was built by the prisoners, with the assistance of the guards. The FAI directs this camp. It is not a prison, nor is it maintained like a garrison. There is no forced labour. Nothing is enclosed and there is no limitation of movement. The prisoners move about freely. Their guards share their life with them, living the same as the prisoners and sleeping on similar cots in the primitive rooms. They address each other informally, as equals. Prisoners and guards are comrades. Neither wears a uniform. They cannot be distinguished by their external appearance.

A young man is standing in front of one of the dormitories. I question him without knowing whether he is a prisoner or a guard.

'I am a prisoner. My name is Benedicto Valles. I belonged to the Acción Popular (Popular Action, a fascist party). That is why I was arrested.'

'How long have you been here?'

'Three months.'

He was not working. He was not feeling well.

'Did the doctor give you permission not to work

today?'

'There is no doctor. The comrade guard gave me permission not to work.'

'Can you receive visitors?'

'Yes. My fiancé comes to see me every Sunday.'

'Can you speak to her alone?'

'Of course. Then we go for a walk together, in the fields.

'Without a guard?'

'Without a guard.'

All the prisoners are permitted to receive visits from their families every Sunday. They are given passes for the camp and surrounding fields. There is no sexual torture that so many prisoners experience in other countries. This is an achievement not to be found anywhere else in the world. The anarchists of the FAI are the first to introduce this humane reform.

Why are there still concentration camps? Because the war against fascism is not yet over; the anarchists must protect themselves against the fascists.

There are chickens, pigs and rabbits in the barns. Cattle are to be seen in the fields. There is one scarcity: water. This vital liquid is not to be found in the entire area. Tank carts must bring it in. Scarcity of water is a great problem here as in other parts of Spain. The soil must be irrigated. Prisoners and guards do this work. One hundred and eighty prisoners work alongside one hundred and twenty-five workers of the collective of Alcañiz to install irrigation. The work is the same for the free workers as for the prisoners. Fascists and antifascists work nine hours a day. They work for the fertility of the soil, to bring new life to the country. The canal must be finished in two years.

The Municipal Council in Alcañiz has taken charge of the work. There is no support from the State or the provincial authorities. The work is being done without engineers. A young peasant who knows how to calculate what must be done to create a self-flowing canal directs the work. The water must come from the Guadalupe River. Some potato fields are already being irrigated.

The CNT and the FAI in Alcañiz initiated this work. Fascists and anti-fascists are working together for the cultivation of the Aragón desert.

There are concentration camps in the fascist countries, Italy and Germany. In the Hitler camp at Oranienberg, the spiritual German poet, (Eric) Muehsam, was assassinated after being tortured and martyred for more than a year. Dozens of known political figures and people who love liberty languish in the concentration camps of National Socialism. The democracies, faced with the alternative of choosing National Socialism and fascism or anarchism, choose the first. They ought to visit the concentration camp in Germany, and then the FAI camp at Valmuel. There: barbarism; here: fighters for liberty.

Calanda

A granite fountain has been constructed in the village square in front of the church. The initials of the CNT and FAI are engraved at the base. The former church is now a warehouse. The sales departments are not yet finished. The butcher shop, newly installed in an annex of the church, is elegant and hygienic, nothing like it known in the village until now. Purchases are not made with money. No money is paid for supplies or services. The women receive meat for vouchers. They belong to the collective and this is enough to obtain food.

The village has no money. It does not require any. The militia comes to the union office of the National Confederation of Labour (CNT) to buy postage stamps. They pay their money. The collective then takes the letters to the Committee where they are mailed.

The village, with a population of 4,500, is located in the district of Alcoriza. The CNT is the dominant group. Seven hundred wage earners belong to it. The collective has 3,500 members — the remainder are individualists. There is no FAI group. The Libertarian Youth (FIJL) has 180 members. A number of UGT members and Left Republicans organised themselves during the past month.

The village is rich, clean and friendly. They have 23,000 pesetas in the treasury. The village produces olive oil, wheat, potatoes, wine and fruit. The principal exports are olive oil and fruit. The annual production of olive oil is 1,750,000 kilos. Large landowners controlled everything until they lost their property July 19th. Collectivists and individualists live side by side in peace. There are two cafes in the village, one for the individualists, and the other for the collectivists. They enjoy the luxury of coffee every evening. The peasants come to the brightly lit room, decorated with CNT and FAI posters, and drink coffee. They read newspapers; some play dominoes, others chess.

The barbershop is a fraternal expression of the collective spirit. Peasants were never shaved before. Now, almost all have well-shaved faces. The services of the barbershop are free. Everyone can have a shave twice-a-week. With twelve modern barber chairs in a well-lit shop, service is satisfactory and hygienic.

Each person is given five litres of wine per week. There is no shortage of food. There is also cloth and clothing. Forty persons a day receive different articles of clothing. A list has been prepared to assure a turn to all. An exchange of olive oil with a textile factory in Barcelona has been arranged.

Work is intensive and there are not enough hands. Five hundred young men, all members of the CNT, are at the front fighting against fascism. The fascists in the village did not put up a resistance. Collectivisation was established during the first days after July 19th. Everything was collectivised here except for the small storekeepers who wanted to maintain their independence. The pharmacy belongs to the collective, as does the doctor. He receives no money and is supported like other members of the collective.

The Municipal Council has six members, four from the CNT, two from the Libertarian Youth. The latter are particularly active, having built public baths and created a library. They conduct meetings and arrange cultural evenings. The cinema is collectivised.

The school, attended by 1,233 children, is the outstanding program in the village. It follows the philosophy and the guidelines of Francisco Ferrer. The school building, an old convent, had 8 teachers before. The CNT brought in 10 more teachers. The relationship between teachers and pupils is magnificent. Teaching methods are modern and the results are extraordinary. The school has a farmhouse. It provides a meal for children of the militia who are at the front. Gifted children, twelve or fourteen of them, are sent to the Lyceum at Caspe, with costs covered by the collective.

Individualists also benefit from the collective. The small proprietors who do not understand its advantages are respected. They pay no rent and receive free electricity from the village's waterfall-powered generator. The members of the collective are content. The peasants are better off now than when April, May, and June were months of hunger. Their standard of living is improved. All the artisans are collectivised. A small stock of cattle remains the private property of the peasants, and every peasant has a pig in the pigsty.

There used to be a branch of a bank in the village. Today it is closed. Seventy thousand pesetas were seized. It was taken over by the municipality that buys supplies with these funds.

The peasants work in groups of ten. The land is divided into zones. Each group, headed by a delegate, works its zone. The groups are formed by friends.

There is a great spirit of solidarity among the people. They are not thinking of acquiring money and goods privately, for themselves. Even the militia do not send money to their families, but to the collective. They are one great family and each is concerned for all.

Alcoriza

Jaime Danden Segovia is a lawyer who practises in Saragossa. He is a native of Alcoriza where his family has a home in the country. His liberal convictions attracted him to the village. He has been living in Alcoriza the last few years, helping the Labour Movement in their cultural activities.

July 19th was for him, as for many others, the beginning of a new life. Egoism is the key to action. Voluntarily, Jaime Segovia placed his lands at the disposition of the collective. He joined the organisation and helped create the structure of the collective. He began to live like a proletarian. He worked tirelessly to build the new society. Now he works as a teacher in the 'Ferrer Guardia' school of the Municipality.

After July 19th, eight comrades conceived the plan to create a collective. The idea spread rapidly among the residents of the village.

Alcoriza was a confederal (CNT) village for some time. The CNT has been in the community since the proclamation of the Republic. When the miners of Figols proclaimed libertarian communism in 1932, there were repercussions in this village. On December 8 1933, when Gil Robles became Minister of War, Alcoriza led the insurrectional movement in Aragón. Of the 4,000 residents,

3,700 are members of the collective. The others remain individualists.

The only organisations in the community are the CNT, the FAI and the Libertarian Youth. The main work is the cultivation of wheat and olives. Green vegetables are also grown for export. There are no unemployed and 300 comrades from the area are at the front.

The system of distribution seems to be somewhat complicated to a stranger. There are vouchers and consumer cards as in other villages, but accounts here are kept by points, with a point having a value of seven *centimos*. This calculation is applied for products that are rationed because of scarcity. Bread, wine and green vegetables are distributed without limit. One hundred-and-fifty grams of meat per person are issued daily. The peasants still keep a small stock of cattle privately, but they have been distributed equitably among all families. Each family has a right to have a pig, each person two chickens and as many rabbits as they wish.

Starting in October, the collective has been keeping records of everything it buys and sells outside the village. Up to January 1 1937, income from the sale of produce amounted to 377,572 pesetas, with expenses at 284,793 pesetas. At the end of the year, the collective has more than 93,000 pesetas in the treasury. During the first three months of 1937 the volume of commerce outside the village increased. Income amounted to 693,000 and outgo 698,000 pesetas. The amount in the treasury remained approximately the same, but the standard of living of the people is higher. These figures do not include the value or volume of barter exchange with other localities.

The collective of Alcoriza has distinguished itself for

its special economic initiative. They established a sausage factory in an old convent, with daily production reaching 500 kilos. This production is sent to the anti-fascist militia. They have also built a shoe factory where they produce leather and fabric footwear, not only for the residents of their village, but also for neighbouring communities. The daily production quota is100 pairs of sandals, and 40 to 50 pairs of shoes. In a new factory for chemical products, they produce cleansers, mineral waters and soda water. This factory also serves the needs of all the villages in the district.

There is an ongoing legal dispute with the neighbouring village of Albalate el Luchador where the electrical plant that supplies Alcoriza is located. The plant is also collectivised and is run by the CNT-UGT collective. This collective demands payment for electricity at the old rate, which the community of Alcoriza does not accept. They want to contribute their share of the wages, the cost of maintenance, etc., but not more. The legal suit has not been settled yet.

The collectivised tailor shop of the village is located in the convent. No wages; the tailors belong to the collective. The collective works on fabrics and materials free of charge.

'Isn't there too long a wait,' I ask, 'for a suit or a dress?'

'No,' answers one of the tailors. We are able to satisfy all orders.'

'Are you satisfied with the new social order?'

'Yes. We have work all year round now. In the past we had nothing to do for three or four months each year. This is changed. Consumption has increased. There is plenty of work. The members of the collective can dress better.'

The village had no restaurant, but the collective has installed a collective kitchen in the old convent. The Committee issues vouchers to outsiders for payment for a meal in the collective kitchen. The food is good and healthy.

The Libertarian Youth have built a library and a community centre. As in the majority of the towns, the youth are the heart and soul of the cultural aspirations of the collective.

Six hundred children of school age go to the Ferrer Institute. There are a dozen teachers, each with 50 pupils.

A magnificent union headquarters has been built, with meeting halls and offices. The members of the collective are proud of their achievements and are planning to have an exhibition of local industry in one of the halls.

The Municipal Council has 8 members, all of whom belong to the CNT. The members of the Council, except for one, continue to work on the farm or in the shop in their regular trades. Two men were in the office of the collective.

All members of the collective are shaved free of charge in the collectivised barber shop.

The members of the collective are proud of their new cinema, installed in the former church. They point out the frontispiece with the initials of the CNT and the FAI. The church has been transformed for its new role. In place of obscure mysticism, new paintings radiate joy. White cloth-like garments with folds fill the space between the pillars. For better acoustics they separated the upper part of the church from the lower half of the hall. There are three film programmes each week, and a special programme for the children on Saturday afternoons. We attend one of these. Instead of a litany the film presents the song '*Hijos del Pueblo*' (the libertarian song, 'Sons of the People'). A profanation? We, the outsiders, were the only ones in the whole enthusiastic audience to think of this word.

Mas de las Matas

The fascists put up no resistance here. When it became known that the Civil Guard attempted a *coup d'état* under the command of the 'Africans,' the CNT militants of the neighbouring villages met and proclaimed collectivisation together with Mas de las Matas. Although anarchists have been active in this town for 20 years, the CNT was not organised here until 1932.

Food is rationed. Only bread is distributed without limit. Of the 2,300 residents of the village, 2,000 belong to the CNT and 300 to the UGT. Five hundred heads of families, a total of 2,000 people, belong to the collective. The remaining 300 residents are individualists who must pay for things with money. Since there are no private stores and shops, they must buy from the collective where they have a line of credit. Food must be rationed for them also. The individualists bring the product of their labour to the collective and receive merchandise of equivalent value. They can, if they wish, take their goods to the city, but this gives them no line of credit. They prefer to work with the collective. Authority is in the hands of the CNT. There is a Committee of Investigation, but the prison is empty.

The community has a flour mill which produces for its own consumption. A mill worker explains: 'There are too many comrades at the front. We do not have enough hands. Our day begins at five in the morning and ends after dark. But we like to work because we know we are in the fight against fascism.'

Alcohol production for Aragón is located in Saragossa, which is cut off from free Spain. New distilleries have been built in the liberated zone. A small one is located in this village producing 200 litres of alcohol per day, which is shipped to Caspe, provincial capital of free Aragón. The former owner continues to work in the distillery, as does the technical director. A small dress shop employs ten girls who work eight-hours-a-day. Like the mill workers, they are not paid a wage. Formerly they received two pesetas a day. Now, in a socialised economy, they are doing much better. They are clean and well-dressed, and they all know how to read and write. There are no unemployed workers anywhere. The former owner of the shop is as concerned for the work today as in the past. When we visited the shop the workers had already left. However, he was still working. We question him:

'I don't have the burdens and the worries now,' he declares. 'In the past the shop was idle several months a year. Now we work steady through the year. I don't have to worry about getting orders. I have enough to live. The collective takes care of everything. I worked before. I'm still working.'

This former owner took the revolution with equanimity, putting a good face on what could not be avoided.

Collectivisation took place in the town in September 1936. It was done under the law of confiscation of the property of fascists. The collectivity decided to collectivise all private property on the basis of the law. The former owners of shops and plants did not oppose the new order.

The law permitted them to continue to own their property, but they joined the collective voluntarily and turned over their property.

The doctor does not belong to the collective. He is known to have rightist ideas, but his convictions are respected and he continues to practice his profession as previously.

The collective has not yet created new institutions. Their tolerance of the individualists impresses favourably. The individualists are a minority. The collectivists are the majority not only in the town, but also in the entire province. They have the capacity to force the individualists to accept the new economic system. But they have not done so. Membership in the collective is voluntary. Those who wish to remain outside the collective are not condemned. However, the individualists do not have the privilege of hiring people to work for them. They can have as much land as they can cultivate together with the members of their families. They can work for themselves and they have nothing to fear from the collective.

Compared with the collectives, the situation of the individualists is poor. Collective work, collective economy offers advantages to the members of the collective. The individualist must endure difficulties in silence. Many understand this and they join the collective. Only dyed-in-the-wool conservatives are unable to change their attitudes.

The new idea has great suggestive force. The main idea behind collectivisation arises out of the philosophy of anarchism, as does libertarian communism.

Oliete

The town is located on the bank of the Martin River, a tributary of the Ebro River in Teruel Province. In the past almost all of their 2,300 residents were small property owners.

On July 19th, the Guards in the barracks attempted to frighten the town away from revolutionary ideas. The men of the town, especially the known CNT militants, escaped, but returned a few days later, having joined a CNT antifascist column, 'Jover,' and the Civil Guards fled along with a number of the fascists. The barracks of the liberated town were empty. Armed forces have not come to the town since then. Two anarchists who had suffered persecution under Primo de Rivera in the Twenties are the town's organisers. They lived in France as emigrants for many years, returning to the town of their birth shortly before July 19th. Familiar with anarchist doctrine, they knew how to distinguish between different socialist systems and ideologies. Their efforts fell on fertile soil. The ideas of Pi y Margall and Anselmo Lorenzo were known in the town and collectivisation had been studied for many long years. Theory up until then, it was put into practice now.

After the town was freed of the armed fascists, the people voted to abolish 'individualism,' that is, individual labour and consumption. Money was suppressed and the land was divided into zones for the labour groups that were formed. The cattle were left with their owners. The number of cattle in private hands was not large. In some instances the distribution was more just than previously. There is a proposal to establish a large pasture. The new collective system requires the separation of consumption and production. Each must be able to satisfy their needs.

The most important product is olive oil. The distribution in the community is 34 litres of oil per person until the end of the year with potatoes, fruit, and green vegetables distributed freely, without limit. Wine, one litre per day. Everything is free. Every adult has the right to 0.40 pesetas of manufactured goods daily, or 12 pesetas per month. Children under fourteen years of age receive one half of this. The consumer cooperative is located in the former church. A noodle and spaghetti factory has been established in the former sacristy.

We visit the town on Sunday. Everybody was working the fields. The harvest must be gathered in. The community agreed that everybody would work Sundays until these tasks were finished. The church, that is the consumers' cooperative, was open although normally it is closed on Sundays. An examination of the different departments of the cooperative showed a plentiful supply of foods. Nobody was complaining. We speak with the pharmacist: 'People are buying five times as much medicine as before,' he says. 'The people are not stingy where medicines are needed.'

There is not much milk. The town has only fourteen cows. A medical certificate is needed to obtain milk. There are 149 sick people in the town; they receive special rations as prescribed by medical certificate. Exact records of consumption are kept for each resident. The record is entered in each person's consumer book and in the cooperative's books. One can see the exact amount of foods and other necessities each person has received at any time.

Carpenters, metal workers and those in other trades also keep statistics for the use of tools. Socialisation has been fully implemented. The work collective offers a good example of activity.

The town imports 30,000 pesetas worth of commodities each month; its exports have risen to 35,000. The commercial balance is good. Money is kept only for exchange with other localities. There is no payment for schooling, rent or light.

Work in the fields is organised by groups. There is one bell left in the bell tower; the others were removed. The bell calls them to work in the morning and to lunch at midday. Pocket watches were bought for the group delegates to facilitate keeping to schedule.

In the past, the small farmer worked away from home almost six months a year. There was not enough work in the town, and people did not own enough land to sustain themselves. The town lands are sufficient now to feed the entire population. They do not have enough hands because several hundred young men are at the front. The militia also regard themselves as sons of the community and have sent 5,000 pesetas to the collective. They want to send more so that the collective can buy new farm machinery.

The committee members of the collective are enthusiastic anarchists and have shown enormous initiative. Coal was found on the outskirts of the town, which they started to mine immediately. They also ship olive oil to Barcelona.

With the proceeds they purchase machinery, electrical supplies, motors and a water pump. Eighteen young workers work in the mine. They began drawing out coal on January 1st with no engineer or technician to assist them. One of the two emigrants had worked in the coalmines of northern France during his long years of exile and he put his experience to the service of the cause cheerfully. Rails and electricity were installed in the mine and production started within a few weeks. They produce a freight car load per day. Production could be tripled if there were more hands and enough machinery.

Three neighbours were expelled because they criticised everything about the collective constantly. A few days later they asked for readmission.

There is no Municipal Council. The Committee is the ultimate authority. The secretary of the former Mayor is now the Justice of the Peace. On July 19th the CNT was the only organisation in the town. One month later some members of the Esquerra Catalan (Catalan Nationalist Left) organised a UGT union and the CNT put a building at the disposal of the new union. The organisations tolerate each other. In May 1937, when fratricidal strife broke out in Barcelona, a member of the CNT Committee was attacked and killed in a street of the town by a member of the UGT. The assassin fled. The CNT closed the headquarters of the UGT and almost all of its members returned to the CNT, to which they had belonged before. Now the CNT is the only organisation in the town.

The FAI had groups in the town and the Libertarian Youth has 130 members. The Youth Organization has its headquarters in the former town hall. They have a community centre and a library. The prison is empty and is used for storing construction materials. There are no armed guards. The military front is 50 kilometres to the west but the people have peace in their community, remain vigilant in defence of liberty and work for their wellbeing.

The collective adopted a resolution on April 22nd defining relations between members of the collective and individualists:

> 1) The Committee, with the agreement of the organisations, resolves: Any comrade who is dissatisfied with the Collective is free to withdraw and to work his land privately as an individual with the understanding that he cannot have more land than he can cultivate himself and that exploitation of man by man will never be permitted to return.
>
> The individualist comrades shall abstain from working against the collective or they will be judged as counter-revolutionaries.
>
> 2) The collectivists shall respect the individualists.
>
> The active comrades of the two central organisations, CNT and UGT, in view of their collectivist principles, will do everything possible to support the collective.
>
> 3) Relations between collectivists and individualists shall be as follows:
>
> The Cooperative and the Collective shall open a line of credit for each individualist for the value of the commodities he brings in. The

individualist can buy from the inventory of the collective with the credit he has established provided the merchandise is not needed by the collective.

The cattle of individualists can graze anywhere in the municipality always respecting the cultivated areas and not exceeding 25 head of cattle per person. The pastures must be respected and preserved by the individualists.

Any reduction of the herds that must be made in Oliete because of the war and the proximity of the town to the front lines, will be shared proportionately by the collective as follows: the existing herd will be divided into three categories: good, medium, poor. It will then be divided proportionately among the owners of the cattle in accordance with the three categories, openly and above board.

4) One of the more interesting aspects of protecting the economy of the community is the supervision and control of the cattle belonging to the individualists by members of the Municipal Council, the Commissioner of Health, a UGT member, and the Commissioner of Cattle, a CNT member.

If the harvest reaped by the individualists from their cultivated lands is squandered or sabotaged, the two members of the Council have the authority to take over the property of the individualist saboteurs.

5) The membership of both organisations will

be checked by four comrades of the UGT and four of the CNT named at open meetings.

Muniesa

The Morella Column drove the fascists out of town August 5th and the town was then collectivised, with everyone joining the collective. Only seven people, functionaries of the State and public authority, are not members of the new community. However, they are linked to the life of the town economically. The town has only 1,700 residents. There were more before July 19th, but a number left with the fascists. The Esquerra Republicana (Republican Left) was represented in the town previously, but the CNT is the only organisation in the community today.

The driving force of the collective is a young miller who lived in Barcelona for 17 years. His initiative, intelligence and energy placed him at the head of the organisation. He is President of the CNT and Secretary of the Collective, which is also the Municipal Council.

The Collective and the CNT union are headquartered in the town hall. *The Conquest of Bread* is on the table in the office. Joaquin Valiente, the organiser, took the book as his model. The teacher's theories have been put into practice by the disciple with the complete approval of the town.

He has his own ideas: libertarian communism including the abolition of money. The town has nothing to do with money that loses value. The money issued by the town is not a substitute for the money issued by the State.

The new town money is not an instrument of inflation, but a medium of exchange. Bread, meat, olive oil and wine are distributed free of charge.

We walk through the town one Sunday afternoon. The bakery was open. Anyone can come for whatever bread he wants.

'Are there not abuses of this?'

'No,' answers the old man who gives out the bread. 'Everyone takes as much as they actually need.'

Wine is also distributed freely, not rationed.

'Doesn't anyone get drunk?'

'Until now there has not been a single case of drunkenness.'

This is a magnificent demonstration that liberty educates, does not corrupt. In addition, Spaniards are a temperate, sober people.

Each male worker receives one peseta a day. Children under ten years of age receive 0.50 pesetas. Girls and women receive 0.75 pesetas. This is not a wage. It is distributed together with food so that the people can buy other things. The community has printed 100,000 pesetas. The new currency was introduced only one month ago. 11,000 pesetas have been put in circulation up to now. As necessary, the community pesetas are exchanged for the national currency. However, there must be a valid reason, such as the purchase of things not available in the town, or the need to take a trip.

The prison is empty with no guards or armed police. The people are peaceful. No one bears arms. Only one person has been nominated by the Municipal Council to be responsible for public order. He does not wear a uniform. There has not been a single conflict, robbery or crime in the town since the collective came into being. Culturally, the town is worse off than other communities. There is not a single teacher. Five hundred children cannot go to school. Illiteracy is widespread. There is no cinema, nor is there is no doctor in the town. Two residents with some knowledge of teaching do what they can, however poorly.

On Saturday and Sunday coffee is served free of charge to everyone in town. People gather in the town hall where coffee is served. Women rarely join them. They never went to the cafe before and it is not the thing to do in the towns.

A Regional Assembly

Until now, Workers' Assemblies could deal with socialism only in theory. Socialism was something that ought to be. Reality was different. Theory was not part of life, had no force. The capitalist social order was the political and economic order.

Now it was different. Delegates of the free communes met in the small city of Híjar – 4,500 residents and general headquarters of the CNT columns. There was no discussion of theory, only of community practice. The seizure of the land and the means of production described by socialist theorists as the final phase of the struggle and the precondition for the realisation of socialism has been accomplished here.

What must be done now? Concern about this was characterised as utopian by learned Marxists, like burying one's head ostrich-like in the sand. Programmes for socialist reconstruction Utopian? But utopia must become reality sometime or the theory would only be another utopia. The utopians proved themselves to be the realists at this point with the economy of liberated Aragón in their hands. The land, the factories and everything produced are the property of the collective, of all the workers. Anarchist communism is the creative idea: exchange, distribution. There are still individualists who prefer to work alone, for themselves, instead of joining the collective and working collectively. The Congress had to study these problems. The economic collectives are members of a federation that groups producers together regardless of affiliation. The parties with authoritarian philosophies, however, continue to seek power for themselves alone.

The actual experience of collectivisation destroyed more than one theory. The unions had to be the bearers of the new life, the anarcho syndicalists pointed out. Unions, the organisations of defence against capitalism, must be transformed into collectives for production and consumption. The new collectives are not exactly identical with the former unions. The CNT must continue. It cannot allow itself to be absorbed by the collectives. It should orient the collectives; provide them with an ideal, content. The Congress agreed to establish a federation of CNT unions. The economic centre of Aragón must be the Federation of Collectives and it must remain independent and not be controlled by any party or organisation.

Classes no longer exist in Aragón now. This is emphasised by the speakers. But the State must also disappear together with classes. The collectives do not want the central State to meddle in their economic affairs, a viewpoint they share with the unions. The practical problems of the Congress were resolved: agricultural machinery, sale of agricultural produce, and formalising relations with the individualists. It is characteristic of the collectives that they do not want to use force against the individualists. They are seen as defenders of capitalist immorality who do not understand the high ideals of brotherhood and solidarity. However, the collectivists do not want to compel them to take the road to liberty.

The great difference between bolshevism and

anarchism, between state and libertarian communism, is based on this. The social movements of our times have not understood this difference. But the time is not far off when it will be understood.

Azuara

When Buenaventura Durruti advanced through Aragón with the anti-fascist columns, taking towns and cities, his arrival was greeted as the liberation of the people not only from the claws of fascism, but also from capitalism. The war against fascism was also the revolution, the transformation of the capitalist economic system into another, more just system. The revolution was much more profound in the war zone of Aragón than in the rear. The process was precisely the goal and the motivation of the antifascist struggle. The town of Azuara is located in the middle of the war zone, six kilometres from the front. It looks like a military encampment with the Red and Black Column having established its barracks there. In the past there was no CNT organisation in the town only one UGT local union. Then an anarcho-syndicalist union was organised which took away almost all of the UGT members. There is a Libertarian Youth organization to which many of the militia belong.

We attend a CNT assembly one Saturday evening. A new member of the Committee must be elected. Condition: he must be able to read and write, and have been affiliated to the organisation prior to July 19th 1936. Mothers are at the meeting with babies nursing at their breasts. Large and small problems of the collective are dealt with. They are satisfied with the distribution of bread, olive oil, potatoes and beans. But there is not enough wine. There was enough clothing for distribution to the members of the collective during the first six months. The meeting goes on record as satisfied with the distribution of vouchers: a married couple 1.75 pesetas daily, children 8 to 15 years of age 0.75, and children younger than 8, 0.50 pesetas.

There are no complaints about hours of work. They cannot be reduced while the war continues. They have no problem with transportation, doctors, medicine or agricultural machinery. The antifascist column provides these to the town. The town pays for them with tobacco and wheat.

A new distribution of work groups is discussed. Some of the young people have to give up their jobs because they are being transferred to other sectors of the front. Collectivisation has been extended to include members of the UGT. They also belong to a new economic community and the collectives have a coordinating committee.

Incidentally, there are no priests or fascists in the town. Unfortunately, the children cannot go to school. War makes stable school life impossible. Enemy planes bomb the town frequently.

Many members of the militia are at the meeting. There is a cordial relationship between them and the people in the town. The Libertarian Youth have established a library. The faces of the militia reflect their idealism.

Formerly the priest performed all the marriages. Now the young people go to the Municipal Council or the union for the ceremony. The church is a garage serving the townspeople and the militia.

The Regional Committee of twelve towns is located in Azuara. They send delegates who report what each town can deliver and what they need. The Regional Committee maintains statistics and products are exchanged between the communities on the basis of the data. The new economic system, a system of organised exchange or barter, has encountered no difficulties until now. There is only a shortage of working hands.

The collectives do not suffer a lack of daily newspapers. They read more than ever before. The Town Committee receives papers from the cities and distributes them among the comrades. At night the collectives gather at the union hall to read the press. They have left the old cafe: the collectivists, puritanical, see it as a frivolous institution.

Valderrobres

The communist system strangles people's economic initiative. It puts brakes on all progress. This is a principal argument of the defenders of private property and capitalist forms of production. Until now the collectivist could answer this only theoretically. There was no actual example anywhere to be able to observe how it affects individual initiative. Russia cannot be cited in this regard. The Stakhanovist movement demonstrates the degree to which workers can develop competence. There are as many different wage levels in Russia as in other capitalist countries. A truly communist economic system is characterised by equality of consumption: each consumes according to his needs. And where need exceeds the capacity to produce they work to increase production. That is what is happening in the libertarian collectives in Aragón.

Initiative? A stranger can appreciate the initiative of the people in the town of Valderrobres. There are groups of houses on the mountain slopes arising from the valley of the Matarrana River. Some of the residents decided to paint their houses sky blue. Others followed their example. The entire town now shines with sky blue homes. Beceite has also been painted the same colour. A romantic dream such as Eichendorff might imagine in his *Life of a Vagabond*.

The landscape changes as we advance. The desolation

of the bare Aragón hills disappears as if by enchantment. The scene changes to a fertile valley of olive trees on the banks of the river.

A collective has been established here in Valderrobres. There was a struggle when the Civil War broke out. Twenty well-armed Civil Guards and a large group of fascists attacked the town on July 19th. The people, deprived of arms, withdrew toward the nearby Catalan frontier where they joined the CNT columns advancing from Tortosa. They were given arms and went looking for the enemy. The battle took place near Villalba de los Arcos. The antifascists won and the fascists withdrew toward Calaceite. They were followed and, on July 27th, 1,000 men of the FAI and the CNT attacked and defeated them. The Civil Guards retreated from Calaceite, which had hitherto been regarded as impregnable. Teruel Province was free of all reactionary forces.

Valderrobres, capital of the district with a population of 3,700, has a long revolutionary tradition. They proclaimed libertarian communism in December 1933, but reaction triumphed. Three days after their ephemeral victory, liberty was drowned in blood. It was different this time. Nineteen towns in the district met on August 9 1936 and agreed, in a regional assembly, to establish collectives. Libertarian communism was created in the collectives with Communism developing furthest in the towns of Mazaleón, La Fresnada, Torre Libre and Beceite. Collectivisation was achieved within two weeks. There was no opposition anywhere. Months later a few individuals asked for the right to work individually and were given permission to do so.

The regional federation is a good example. It

provides statistics on the economic capacity of the collectives in the affiliated towns. It has taken a new census of
the population. It controls the size of the herds of cattle
and their sanitary condition. It has defined the relation-
ships of the political parties and the unions, and between
the members of the collectives and unaffiliated individualists.

Statistics on the harvests make possible accurate
calculations of the economic resources of the town. The
olive harvest this year is worth 30,000,000 pesetas. The
almond harvest was poor because of the frosts. The town
is rich in olives of superior quality.

The Regional Committee consists of delegates of the
affiliated towns. Their work deserves praise. They have
improved means of communication. The Committee has
installed telephone lines between the towns. There were no
telephones in a number of the towns before collectivisation.

The regulation of private property in agriculture in
the different towns used to fill books of registry and
required the services of a great many shyster lawyers. Now
it is handled simply. Under the regime of private property,
municipalities worked hard to incorporate as much property as possible. The collective put an end to taxes among
other difficulties. There are no taxes now. Communities are
not interested in possessing more land. They only want as
much as their residents can work. The town of Valderrobres encompassed lands previously belonging to the
community of Beceite. The two towns entered into an
agreement and Valderrobres returned these lands to the
neighbouring community. Territorial boundaries of a
municipality have only platonic significance. There is no

lack of land and there are no territorial conflicts between communities. When a community forms new labour groups they have enough land at their disposal. A profound transformation has taken place in the thinking of the farming population. The majority of the people of Valderrobres were small farmers. They had always thought in terms of private property. According to the experience of other countries, small peasant proprietors are opposed to the collective ownership of the land. But the farmers gave up private property here. The former private owners continue to work on the land they formerly owned. But they do not work alone; other members of the group help them now.

The collective uses a worker card. Every Saturday, the work done during the week is recorded. Their method of control of distribution of clothing is original: they have a type of wall newspaper in the union hall which reports the amount of clothing and other articles to be issued to each member of the collective. Everyone in the town knows in this way what is being issued to his neighbours.

The members of the collective are dissatisfied with the schools. They want to establish a modern school, like the Ferrer schools. Fifty per cent of the town is illiterate and there are not enough teachers. There is only one school in the district for children. Children are separated by sex starting at six years of age. (This is not happening in Calanda, where children of both sexes attend the same classes.) A professor comes to the town from Tortosa and gives a lecture while we are there. The farmers ask for more teachers to provide free instruction to all their children. The farmers discuss the economic aspects of the matter with the professor.

'You will receive as much as the doctor: food, clothing and all the necessities of life. There is no money in our town.'

The teacher accepts the offer.

Beceite

In 1919, a very energetic Director General of many coal-mines in Silesia committed suicide. He was afraid that the Government of People's Councils would expropriate the mines and he could not accept such a prospect. He explained his motives in a letter to the miners who worked for him: 'Death rather than socialism.'

There are other types of property owners and capitalists. The former owner of two paper mills in Beceite did not think of killing himself when the new era began. He adapted himself to the new reality and manages his factories as he did before. Dressed only in his shirt and pants, he works at the machines together with the workers in the collectivised shops, using his technical knowledge with the same interest as in the past. Does he think of the 'good times' of the past when he is alone? He has no income or amenities of life other than the members of the collective. He appears to be calm and undisturbed. He sings at his work when he thinks he is not observed.

Production of paper is a little lower than before. There is a lack of raw material. The factory produces a fancy paper.

In the past smokers had to buy their tobacco. Now the members of the collective receive their tobacco free. There is a special book for smokers. The community has 1,579 residents, 231 adult men and 207 smokers. Each smoker receives four packages of cigarettes per week.

'How do you supply the people with clothes?'

'Everyone has a card with a number.'

I see a woman ask for two shirts for her husband and her son. The 'bureaucrat' looks up number 315. Two months ago she received two shirts, but it is not enough. She can have two more.

'And cloth for a dress for my daughter?'

She can have that also.

The woman then goes to the cooperative with her requisitions. They give her what she needs.

Individualists must buy what they want. Some pay with money; others charge it against produce that they will deliver later. Prices are low.

It is eleven o'clock in the morning. The gong sounds. Mass? It is to remind the women to prepare the midday meal.

Calaceite

The supporters of private property are against collectivisation. They defend the old privileges based upon property.

There was a time when technical progress and free collaboration between groups was resisted. Small business saw only dangerous competition in big business. Large scale mechanised production created a wealth of industrial products.

Agricultural production has not moved forward for a hundred years. In large agricultural enterprises (within the capitalist system) workers are merely servants. It is significant that the term 'servants' continues to be used in agriculture.

Collectivisation has all the advantages of free cooperation: humane collective labour. Freedom and equality are its foundation. An ox and a horse hitched together to a plough will not cooperate with each other. Cooperation must be based on agreement arrived at freely. The Aragón collectives are economic communities, organised by free and voluntary agreement among its participants. The system of individual labour in agriculture is irrational. In the future they will wonder how early farmers saw themselves.

In capitalist countries a town is not a cohesive working community. It appears to be a number of people brought together in one place by accident, through destiny, war, or a hundred other coincidences. Frequently, the citizens have nothing in common. Sometimes relatives get together. However, their economic interests may be in conflict. They are opposed to each other, and private property is the issue that separates them. They compete in the sale of their products. They do not work together, but against each other. Production and the entire economy suffer under the weight of these discrepancies. The economy in these towns is irrational. Progress has passed these fields by. Workers are excluded from the management of production in the large agricultural properties under capitalism. The means of obtaining wealth are in the hands of the employers, the tools as well as the slaves. Freedom and dignity are suppressed.

The farmers of Calaceite understand all this. They modernised their agricultural enterprises. Three thousand people live in this town, most of them small farmers, a few blacksmiths, a few carpenters, each working in their own small shop. They used to work in primitive ways, without machinery. The collective showed them the way to work together. Now they have a large machine shop; ten men work there in clean, healthy surroundings. All the carpenters in the town work together in a large woodworking shop.

The town is organised today. It constitutes a large working community. There are twenty-four labour groups with twenty competent workers in each group. They work the community's fields together according to goals set in advance. In the past everyone worked for himself; today they work for all. Cattle breeding is organised along modern lines. Large herds of livestock are established. In the past the peasants had no land; now all the land in the community belongs to them. They did not have enough workers. Now the country can feed more people. This is the meaning of collectivism.

The town has two pharmacies and a doctor. They are part of the collective. There were not compelled to join but did so voluntarily. The bakers opposed the collective. They did not want to join the collective or work under the new conditions. They left the town. Other bakers were not sought. They found a temporary solution: the women baked bread as in the old days. The town would like to have other bakers.

The town, once poor, is satisfied today. Many were hungry in the past; today everyone has enough to eat.

Mazaleón

After July 19th the CNT-FAI Committee in Tortosa invited the people to respect all art objects and to bring them to the Committee. They established a museum with the collection. The anarchists and libertarian youth in many cities and towns in Spain were the protectors of the cultural riches in their communities. Abroad, Spanish workers and peasants, and especially the anarchists, were characterised as barbarians, destroyers of all cultural life.

A town on a mountain ridge, dominated by the church built centuries ago as an expression of collective life. The peasants went to church as a place to meet where they were all united by a common idea. All of them had the same concerns, the same aspirations, and the same cultural conception: the instinct of race, the sense of a universal order in the work induced the peasants to make a collective effort to build the church.

Things have not changed at Mazaleón up to now. The spirit remains the same; the form has changed. The mysticism of the Catholic Church is no longer there. The priests have disappeared. But the peasants do not work to destroy this Gothic building that majestically crowns the peak of the mountain. They have transformed it into a cafe and a lookout site; a nice place to have meetings. They have modernised the buildings and installed loud speakers. They do not meet there Sunday mornings for prayer. Now they meet Sunday afternoons in their collective house under the high Gothic arched roof. The comrades are positivists: they want to enjoy life and nature. They have opened wide the windows of the church. They have set up a large gallery where the altar once stood. The view embraces the southern slope of the Aragón Mountains; a setting of tranquillity, reflection. Neighbours gather there on Sunday, take their coffee and enjoy the calm of the afternoon.

Belief in nature has taken the place of religion, which has been banished. Something more noble has been born: the belief in man and his collective. This is the religion of the Mazaleón peasants today. Everything is collectivised here. Collectivisation was voted unanimously. The teachers also belong to the collective, although they are paid by the State that is not part of the economic community of the town.

'What do you think of collectivisation?'

Bautista Domingo, schoolteacher, socialist and in disagreement with the anarchist ideology and movement, replies:

'I regard collectivisation as great progress. I have been living in collectivised towns for several months. The peasants are better off, production has increased, labour has improved the spirit and solidarity is stronger.'

The president of the town collective, Manuel Aranda, had an original idea. He proposed a system of coupons as a substitute for money. His proposal was accepted.

A book of coupons has a value of 25 pesetas. This money is not distributed as wages: it is used solely as a medium of exchange. Every member of the collective receives a book of coupons. He can buy what he needs from the collective's stores; one peseta per day for adults,

75 *centimos* for minors under 14 years of age.

The town's lands are very large. They included, at one time, the property of other villages. Property in the old sense no longer exists. No tax is paid to a municipality. Work groups choose the land they wish to cultivate without investigating first to which town the land belongs. The struggle for property is over. The collective spirit has replaced this irrational conflict.

Albalate de Cinca

Theme: 'The poor are better off now.'

There used to be many rich people in the town and they opposed collectivisation. But they are a minority. The majority of the town has gained material and cultural benefits from collectivisation. A number of women wait at the entrance to the town with large baskets to carry their purchases. They are waiting for the cooperative store to open; they are not accompanied by a Committee member.

The women are unhappy about a number of things. Not enough soap or coffee. Other things are lacking. But this is due to the war. One woman says: 'We have everything in abundance that we need for our daily lives, bread, meat, wine, vegetables. It was not always like this, before collectivisation we were poor.'

A woman of a peasant family summarised their attitude about collectivisation with these important words about the new organization of work: 'WE POOR ARE BETTER OFF TODAY.' No other statement can describe collective work better.

The Town Committee meets in the former city hall. The CNT and the FAI are the only organisations in the town; there are no disagreements between the Municipal Council and the leadership of the organisations. The same people serve in both organisations. An anarchist who lived in France as an immigrant during the dictatorship is President.

A woman wants to go to Lerida to consult a medical specialist. She came to the office at 7 o'clock in the morning. The Committee does not schedule many hours at the office. The Committee members work in the fields together with their groups. They do the work of the Municipality and the organisation in the little free time that remains to them.

'You must obtain a certificate from a doctor to get money for the trip,' the President explains to the woman. The answer does not satisfy the old woman. She complains of rheumatism and tries to convince the Committee to give her the money without a doctor's note, but she does not succeed.

'There are people,' the President explains, 'Who try to take advantage of the new possibilities offered by the collective. Many have never gone to the city. There are elderly neighbours in our village who know nothing about the city except as a collector of taxes. Now that it is possible to travel free of charge, they exaggerate a little.'

The President may have been prejudiced in his explanation. The doctor can give a more objective opinion in this matter.

The doctor, José Maria Pueyo, has lived in the village for twelve years. He has left-wing ideals, but does not belong to any party and he is not an anarchist. A visit with him could be particularly interesting.

Jose Maria Pueyo, a man of mature years, is a native of Saragossa and knows well the peasants of Aragón. There used to be a type of community health insurance. Clients paid the doctor a fixed fee per year. The doctor took care of their major and minor illnesses. When the village was collectivised the former system could not be maintained. The villagers had no money. But the doctor remained in the community and placed himself at the disposal of the collective.

'How is life under the new conditions?'

The collective gives me food, clothing and whatever else I need without difficulties.'

'What about medications and instruments?'

He opened the door of the adjacent building and showed me the stock of medications provided by the collective.

'They are eager to give me everything I need. Sometimes it is necessary to go to Barcelona to get a few things. But they almost always send it.'

The people go to the doctor more frequently than they used to. The poor peasants and day workers could not pay the annual fee for the doctor in the past, under capitalism. They could consult the doctor very infrequently; their situation is better now with the collective.

'Are there abuses?'

'Yes, but it is understandable. The majority could not afford the luxury of a medical examination, or many other things. Today they can, so they exaggerate.'

'What about the problem of senility?'

'In the past the village did not know of a single case. (The village has two thousand inhabitants.) Now, since the outbreak of the war, we have two cases.'

'In my opinion,' said Dr. Pueyo, concluding the interview, 'collectivisation and libertarian communism are a better, more just system than private capitalism. But it must be made more uniform. Most of the difficulties today are due to the fact that there is no unification yet.

Private capitalism still continues in the cities. Money is needed for everything there. And each village has a different medium of exchange that is not recognised anywhere else. This causes many inconveniences. If the system covered the entire country, it would certainly solve Spain's social problem.'

There is no local money in Albalate. The people obtain everything free, through vouchers. Goods are rationed. The consumption of meat is greater today than formerly, although there are no exact statistics. But there is meat now for all the 'sick.' And more is being produced than consumed.

They performed an act of solidarity with Madrid during the month of March, sending the following to the unconquered city: ten live hogs, each weighing 115 to 120 kilos; 500 kilos of bacon; 87 chickens; 50 rabbits; 21½ tons of potatoes; 200 dozen eggs; vegetables and several dozen goats. It was a generous act of solidarity by the town for the people in the capital – j with no question of payment or requisition by the military.

The Regional Committee in Albalate also sent ten truckloads of wheat and other necessities to Madrid as a contribution, without compensation. Convoys of trucks loaded with food from many towns and villages move to the Spanish capital.

The committee provided some statistics as follows: the collective has 113 families with 450 people; 300 work in agriculture. Twenty-five blacksmiths, locksmiths, carpenters, etc. work at their trades. The town has 3,900 hectares of land, of which 800 hectares are dry. 1,800 hectares of cultivated land are irrigated, 500 are dry. The latest crops were 69,000 kilos of wheat, 2,000 kilos of barley, 3,000 kilos of oats, more than 16 tons of potatoes, 4,000 kilos of vegetables and 4,000 of corn. Two hundred hectares were set aside for the cultivation of beets. The increase of production since collectivisation is 15% for wheat, 25% and 30% for potatoes and corn, respectively. The town has 13 oxen, 45 cows, 1,000 sheep, 200 hogs and several hundred goats.

'We want to continue to increase production,' my informant concludes, 'in order to insure the triumph of the antifascist cause and the libertarian revolution. The more we produce the greater our chances of victory.'

Grañén

The large number of active, capable young people in the village Committees of Collectives is surprising to a stranger. The secretary of the Regional Federation of Grañén is a 22-year-old youth, a member of the Libertarian Youth. He was completing a course as a technician. The revolution came and he was finished with his studies. He was placed at the head of the collective. The administration offices can bear comparison with the offices of any capitalist enterprise. Everything must be taken into account: forecasting, ordering, organising talent, an ability to keep an eye on details while seeing the whole. A large map of the region hangs on the wall, with all its roads, wagon trails, bridges and rivers, hills and dry areas. The young secretary must explain with persuasive clarity the characteristics of the land and its economic possibilities to the peasants who come to the office.

The Grañén region has 27 affiliated collectives with an area of 96,000 hectares. There are 11,600 residents. The Regional Federation manages all interchange among the 27 villages. There are two principal types of operation: a) direct exchange between villages through the Federation; b) the sale of surplus produce and the purchase of necessary goods for the region. The Regional Federation must authorise all exchange between villages and what must be bought from the outside. An example:

'Authorisation:

'Regional Federation of Agricultural Collectives of Grañén.

'This Regional Federation authorises the Sangarren Collective to ship 3,000 kilos of wheat to Lerida, as part of an interchange.

'Grañén, June 3, 1937.'

The Regional Federation received 174,000 tons of wheat during the month of April. The value has not yet been established because prices have been increasing sharply.

The Regional Federation helps all the villages to solve their economic problems. The peasants do not have to cart their produce in with horse and wagon. Instead, the Regional Federation's trucks pick up the produce in the villages. This saves time and labour, as does the establish-ment of stores at the Regional Federation. The peasants will look for what they need at these stores. The individual-ists can buy at local Federation stores. The Grañén Federation, like other federations, has no money. It deals generally in wheat and other agricultural produce.

Grañén is the seat of a military hospital of the 'Jover' Division. The village has 1,200 inhabitants. It is collectiv-ised even though the UGT has 120 members and the CNT only 60, because the idea of collectivisation has also won over the socialists and the left republicans.

The land in Grañén used to belong to large estates. The owners did not live in the village. They lived in the cities on the fruit of the labour of their servants.

There was a struggle for the possession of the village. On July 23rd the fascists took it from Huesca. A day and a half later the columns of the CNT and the FAI arrived.

The fascists withdrew. An assembly of peasants was held immediately and they agreed to collectivise.

The agreement states:

1) Recognising that the harvest is a sacred interest of the workers, all the workers of this village must intensify their daily labour with all necessary energy to make up for the time lost in the revolution as quickly as possible.

2)All the goods and properties of owners who sided with fascism become the collective property of the community under the control of the workers' organisations.

3) The large landed estates located in the township also become the property of the village and the tenants who work the estates must turn over the property to the Village Committee.

4) Individual seizure of property and goods in prohibited.

5) In recognition of the liberating mission of the antifascist militia, the community will give them every facility to carry on the struggle against fascism.

6) The popular police of Grañén are created by decree. They will be under the orders of the Village Committee, protecting the interests of the community and popular justice, punishing banditry and all acts against established order with severity.

7) Any difficulties and misunderstandings arising from the above declarations will be resolved by the Village Committee.

Additional Article. All agricultural machinery is the property of the Village Committee (threshing equipment).

Dictated in Grañén, July 31, 1936. For the Military Committee First Column of the Anti-fascist Militia By Order of M. Trueba ROCA For the Village Committee of Grañén Mariano PINOS.'

Groups organised by the residents of each street in the village perform the work of the Grañén Collective. There are 15 work groups. The Collective distributes food supplies, as in most towns and villages, through the issuance of vouchers. Women are given wine, which is unlike other communities. Bread, meat, oil and potatoes are in sufficient supply. Other foods and necessities of life that are not produced in the village are rationed carefully. The administration of the Collective is composed of four members of the CNT and four of the UGT. The Municipal Council is a separate body, with three members from each union.

Collectivisation resolved a serious problem that could not be solved in a system of private property: the distribution of pasture lands among the different municipalities. The following agreement was entered into among a number of villages in the region on January 3rd:

The villages of LALUEZA, CAPDESASO, ALBERUELA DEL TUVO, MARCEN,

FRAELLA, AND GRANEN adopt the following agreements:

1) After a Commission of each village determines how much pasture land they need for their livestock, the remainder of the land can be used for cultivation.

2) We of Grañén are prepared to give some of our pasture land to the other villages only this year if there is a shortage of good pasture land.

3) Likewise, if the villages of MARCEN and FRAELLA find that they do not have sufficient land, they will be given additional land.

Signed _____

The Regional Federation solved the problem of the distribution of land for cultivation and for pasture by agreement at a public assembly to the satisfaction of the residents of the interested villages.

Barbastro

The larger the town, the less collectivisation; the smaller the village the deeper the communist spirit, the more strongly the new economic forms take root. This fact contradicts Marxist conceptions, which affirm that socialism and communism will first be realised by the masses of the industrial proletariat – then the petty bourgeoisie will come along, and finally the agricultural population. This prophecy is based on the false premise that socialism and communism are only the result of the creation of a proletariat, of poverty, of industrialisation. The Aragón peasants have demonstrated by example that industrialisation is not a prior condition for libertarian communism.

Forms of organisation in the liberated areas range from collectivisation to full communism. In the small towns and villages libertarian communism was realised almost completely. But in Barbastro, with 10,000 inhabitants, the agricultural collective consists of only 150 families and has only twelve homes. Things do not go well for the members, as can be seen at a meeting that we attended by chance.

Work groups are set up. Those who want to work together have the first choice. Groups of 10 to 15 people are formed. Each group elects delegates. There are complaints that they do not have enough machinery.

Workers in other occupations are better off. Construction workers also work as a collective, as do other trades. But the industrial collectives are only work communities. The agricultural collectives are communities of work and consumption. They grind the wheat that they produce and they have their own bakers to make bread. Bread is distributed freely to all the members of the collective. Meat is rationed, 100 grams daily for adults, 50 grams for children. Other agricultural products are distributed in the same way. Rent is paid in Barbastro, but the collective pays it, like the father of a family watching over his sons. Members of the collective receive five pesetas per week for clothing and other necessities. Their standard of living is not very high. They could have a higher income if they looked for work in other industries. But they want to continue in the collective. The harvest is 70 truckloads of wheat. They hope to improve their standard of living with this harvest.

The Collective was organised October 16th. With the help of the municipal authorities the members determined how much land was not in cultivation. These lands were placed at the disposal of the collective, as were farms that belonged to fascists or were cultivated by tenant farmers or day labourers. The life of these tenant farmers or day labourers was miserable. They were not paid a salary. They had to be satisfied with a share of the agricultural crop. They could keep one half of the olive crop. But for this they had to take care of their masters' horses. Most of the time there was no market for the sale of their harvest. They had to sell their olives at a lower price, further reducing their income.

The tenant farmers were behind in their rent a full year. Their debts were wiped out after July 19th. They and the day labourers lost nothing with the abolition of private property. On the contrary they gained a great deal. Both groups have an interest in continuing the new economic structure.

Barbastro is the headquarters of one of the largest Regional Federations. Of seventy villages in the region, forty-seven are collectivised and belong to the Federation. Individualists are an insignificant minority. There are also UGT collectives in some of the villages, but they belong to the CNT Regional Federation as well. The affiliated collectives provide exact statistical data to the Regional Federation. They report the number of inhabitants, the size of the area, the condition of wagons and roads, and the number of animals, produce and productive capacity. They record the number of machines available and the number needed, raw materials, food, clothing, etc. The Regional Federation administers the economic affairs of 15,000 members of collectives. From September 1936, when they started, to April 30, 1937, they collected 3,250,000 pesetas; stock worth approximately 1,000,000 pesetas, credits of 2,500,000 pesetas. The Federation provided the War Department principally with its produce. They were not paid. They therefore were not able to carry out many of their projects, including a detailed plan to install a network of telephones throughout the region. This plan, prepared by the telephone workers' collective of Barcelona would cost 516,000 pesetas. The telephone lines cannot be installed because, as we said, the War Department did not settle its debts to the Federation. They also wanted to install new bus lines and improve trucks, wagons and roads. The work was begun, but there were no funds for this either.

We reproduce a part of the report to the Regional Congress held on May First: 'A bus that starts at the village of Colungo, can maintain communication among the ten villages within a radius of sixty kilometres and a total population of 3,356. Now, each peasant goes to the city on his own, losing much time and wasting precious energy.'

The Regional Federation is a sort of Economics Department. There are Departments of Transportation, Agricultural Production, Food Supplies, etc. The Machinery and Tools Department has the responsibility of providing machinery to affiliated villages. The Regional Federation started with six threshing machines that formerly belonged to the big landowners and it bought two more. They also bought eight harvesters. There are thirty-seven modern ploughs in the region, a tractor, and some other agricultural machines. The Federation sends the machines and skilled operators to the villages that need them. 'What is to be done with machines of individualists (private property owners) that work only a few days during the harvest?' ask representatives of the village of Torres de Alcanadre. 'They must be put at the service of the revolution, that is, of the collectives,' the Congress decides.

The collectivised villagers go to the Regional stores for things they do not have in the villages, from seed to foods. The Regional Federation establishes butcher shops throughout the region.

We are in the no-hunting season, but hunting is going on in the majority of the villages. 'What should we do?' is the question before the Congress. The representatives of the Huescan village of Ponzano declare that they must hunt because the animals are a threat to the crop. The Assembly goes on record: 'Before we are criticised for hunting out of season we must give a good example and not hunt at this time.' The Assembly calls upon all villages to respect the no-hunting season.

The Regional Federation also agreed to establish a fortified defence position and defence capability in all the affiliated collectivised villages. The solidarity of the region with the antifascist militia was not limited to words. On April 25, it contributed thirty-five wagonloads of food, part for Barcelona, part for Madrid. Barbastro sends food continuously to the hospitals in Barcelona.

Barbastro was spared all fighting. There were 400 soldiers in the city's barracks who placed themselves resolutely on the side of the antifascists. The city remained in the hands of the people from the beginning.

The UGT grew briefly after July 19th. Whoever did not have a membership card was considered a fascist, so the petty bourgeoisie joined. Among them were suspicious elements. CNT and the UGT agreed to form a Joint Committee to clear the unions of fascist elements. The UGT had only few members after the cleanup.

Binéfar

On July 20, the fascists fortified themselves in the barracks of the Civil Guard. The workers took the lead in the ensuing struggle. They did not wait for the fascists to attack. With help and arms from Lérida, they attacked the fascist barricades and in one hour the battle was decided in favour of the antifascists. The road was free for social reforms.

On August 28, a village Assembly agreed to abolish private ownership of land. Twelve hundred hectares of land were collectivised, with the land being divided into parcels. Seven work groups cultivate the collectivised land. The group delegates meet each evening at the meeting hall to exchange impressions and benefit from the lessons of experience.

The CNT is the only organisation in this town of 5,000. The town issues vouchers as money. Whatever is produced in the town is distributed freely. In addition, doctor services, the hospital and medication are free. Men receive 2.50 pesetas daily in vouchers, women 1.50 pesetas, and children under age 13 1 peseta. The vouchers can be exchanged in the local bank for the currency of the State. There are 45,000 pesetas worth of vouchers in circulation. The idealism of the people is high and it has drawn in the non-proletarian classes. Some of the teachers who are paid by the State turn over their salaries to the Collective and live like the collectivists in the new economy, without money. Consumption and the standard of living of the people have improved in spite of the war.

From July to September, two truckloads of food were sent to the front daily as a gift from Binéfar, which is also the headquarters of a Regional Federation. Part of the food is sent to the cities under attack by fascism. The community sent 32 truckloads of food to Madrid.

There are not enough workers. Six hundred young men are in the ranks of our army, fighting at the front. There are no police, no armed guards in the town. The barracks are empty and the churches closed. Stores of foodstuffs and city made products have been opened in the town and the neighbouring villages. Collective halls are also being constructed.

The Regional Federation has installed electric lines for light and power. New telephone lines were installed in the villages. Three doctors affiliated with the CNT took the initiative, together with the Municipality, to establish a regional hospital. It cost 100,000 pesetas. Since September, 126 operations have been performed. Previously there was no hospital in the town.

Thirty-one collectivised villages belong to the Regional Federation. There are no functionaries of the State, no railway men, no postal workers, etc. who do not belong to the collectives. Collectivisation embraces the population of the entire district. It signifies progress, liberty, and wellbeing.

Monzón

The residents of Monzón put the former church to an original use. When collectivisation took place in this town of 5,000, the carpenters looked for a large building for the collective shop. The church, which had been abandoned by the priests, was the most adequate. The building has very little left of its former purpose: much construction, clear windows, no images of saints — only the remains of the altar. The organ's chords are not heard, but in their place the sounds of mechanical saws, sanders, drills.

More than twenty carpenters work there. They have never had so good a workshop. Collective work is more productive than the individual work of the past. Another church in the centre of the town has been transformed into a barracks where the militia of the 'Land and Liberty' column are housed. A hospital has been installed in a third church. The three churches have been put to practical use. The collectivist spirit has triumphed. Where mass was read, now the love of fellow human beings prevails. What was formerly mysticism is now concrete wellbeing; a work of profound interior and exterior transformation.

Common interests unite, party politics divide. The residents of Monzón are agreed on economic questions; they have conflicts in politics, and there are discussions between partisans of the UGT and the CNT in the Municipal Council. Each side wants to elect its own candidate as

President. The conflict cannot be solved. It is hoped that the conflict will end when the membership rolls are cleaned up in accordance with their mutual agreement. The UGT bases its claim on a larger membership. The CNT denies this. They maintain that there are a great many fascists enrolled in the UGT. The surprising growth of the UGT has an explanation: all of the petty bourgeois elements who formerly belonged to the various parties have joined the UGT. The Libertarian Youth and the FAI are also represented in the town in addition to the CNT and the UGT.

About 1,000 people, all members of the CNT, have organised a collective. The majority are peasants. Fourteen large estates have been expropriated. Sixty per cent of the population are not yet collectivised. However, some of the individualists are using collective forms of work. They help each other in the cultivation of the land, but they do not participate in a communist life. The CNT collectives have a family income. The work communities of the individualists are production cooperatives only. Consumption is completely separate from production. In the UGT shops individuals are paid a day's wage as previously. A worker with a large family is paid the same as an unmarried worker.

Everything that is produced by the CNT collective is distributed free of charge. Everything else must be paid for. A married couple receives six pesetas a day, children up to fourteen, 1 peseta; from fourteen to sixteen years, 1.50 pesetas. Single people receive four pesetas per day; the collective pays for rent and electricity.

The former bank is the headquarters of the collective. A pile of shares of stock, today useless paper, lies in the corner of the office. There is no money in the vaults earning interest. Vouchers, representing work performed, are the medium of exchange and fulfil the function of money.

The collective is a community of comrades who share the same ideal. It is based on the idealism of its members. The collectivist spirit has replaced the individualist spirit. The collectivists collaborate; work together more than the individualists. The latter have also joined together to form cooperatives. The time of individual isolation has passed. The new era develops under the banner of collectivism and free communism. Nothing will hold it back from its victorious road.

Road to Catalonia

We leave the bare Aragón Mountains. The treeless and fertile valleys are behind us — ahead, Catalonia. In Barcelona the pulse of the revolution reflects all the hopes and aspirations of the entire Spanish proletariat. This city was the heart of the revolutionary movement of Spain for decades. The heroes of the working class lived here, waited here for the great decision.

July 19 came. The hopes placed in Barcelona were not disappointed that day. The proletariat, skilled and experienced in fighting, opposed the fascist hordes. Reaction was conquered. The intervention of the Anarchists was decisive. But the Anarchist movement, faithful to its tradition and ideology, did not want to establish a dictatorship. A new era of freedom began. This was their noble ideal.

But those who were planning new intrigues against the people took advantage of this freedom. The bourgeoisie threatens Barcelona again. Speculation flourishes once more. The former politicians remain. They do not want to know anything about social revolution. The proletariat continues to fight, but the bourgeoisie wants neither collectivisation nor socialism.

The revolutionary achievements of Aragón are almost completely unknown in Catalonia. They do not believe it; they think it is a fantasy. The people of

Barcelona know little about the collectives and the libertarian communism in the country. They distrust. 'Such economic structures are too advanced. The people are not yet ready for libertarian communism.'

This is the opinion of the petty bourgeoisie and all who are influenced by petty bourgeois thinking. The only collectivism they know is producers' cooperatives. But collectivism in Aragón is more than that. It has taken a communalist form. Barcelona does not know what has happened in Aragón. Collectivism in Aragón is voluntary. It is not forced as in Russia. The Aragón collectives practice libertarian communism. Only an outside force can overthrow this system. The collectives will succumb if the National Guard comes to the village, dissolves the Committee, arrest its members, plunder its warehouses and make collective work impossible by restoring private property. But it remains to be seen whether brute force would be able to conquer the new spirit that has developed.

If force will not be used to destroy the collectives, nothing will hold back their continuing development. The new economic system will spread through the entire country. The benefits of collectivisation will be greater as the process of collectivisation moves ahead. Aragón is the first great start of socialisation in all Spain where the principles of social justice are being put into practice for the first time.

But agriculture alone in Aragón is not a complete economic community. Too many products are lacking in the provinces. They must be brought in from outside. Means of exchange are needed. Little money is available. Many communities are poor. Only importing products from the cities and abroad can raise the standard of living.

As long as the war against fascism continues every sacrifice must be made. Only after the war is over will it be possible to improve the standard of living of the peasants in the collectives.

It has been said that the workers in the fields and the industrial workers should prepare themselves before the revolution for the organisation of the new life. The agricultural workers have neither the time nor the possibility for such preparation.

Everything happened after July 19. First the peasants had to take the land from the large landholders and make it part of the community. The peasants are not economists or experts in the social sciences. But they had a general idea how to organise a social community. They did not look for a perfect organization. They started small. Collectivisation moved ahead little by little. Only eleven months have passed. What can such a few months mean in the revolution of a country? It will take years to completely replace the capitalist economic system with the communist system. Soviet Russia, twenty years after the revolution has still not found perfect social forms. It is impossible to expect that a perfect organisation of libertarian communism can be established in Spain in one year. A great deal has been realised in less than one year. It is not Aragón's fault if libertarian communism runs into difficulty. If a similar transformation were achieved in Catalonia and all other parts of Spain the rural population of Spain would achieve material wellbeing in a short time. The misery of the peasants was great. It has not been completely overcome yet.

The field worker is not a professional revolutionary. Like everywhere else the peasants of Spain want freedom and prosperity. These can be won by fighting. Prosperity is not possible so long as the country is under the control of political bosses and the land is the property of the church. There can be no freedom so long as militarists, monarchists or even republican governments oppose it.

Since July 19, the great landed estates have been abolished and oppressive power liquidated. The people are able to breathe. They are organising their lives in complete liberty and they are trying to achieve prosperity through their own labour. But prosperity for a few is not a solution. The Aragón peasants who are fighting for libertarian communism want wellbeing for all. If their progress is not stopped from the outside, their new life will earn the admiration of the world in a few years.

In his utopian novel *Les Pacifiques*, Hans Ryner describes an imaginary country, mentioned by Plato that once lay between Europe and America and then disappeared. The life of the Aragón peasants resembles that imagined land. When you return to Barcelona from Aragón you are filled with nostalgia. You want to return to those peasants who are faithful to nature and pursue the ideals of their heart and mind.

Addendum: Alcampel by Victor Blanco

Alcampel (Huesca) 1880-1936

The village is located at almost the extreme southeast of the province of Huesca, at the first spurs of the Pyrenees, 400 meters above sea level. In 1936, it had 2,600 inhabitants.

The municipality has two zones. To the north the village is circled by olive groves, vineyards and fields planted with cereals. In the south the Aragón-Catalonia canal lined with warehouses cuts the plain called 'La Litera'. The inhabitants speak a mixture of Catalan and local tongues that is difficult for Castilians to understand. I don't want the reader to regard me as a local fanatic. I want to explain liberalism in Alcampel to the best of my ability.

Between 1830 and 1850 (according to stories told for years by my father's grandmothers and others whom I knew up to the time I left for France) it was a woman, Maria del Sabone, who broke the first link of the oppressive chain of religion and established the guidelines to be followed. Nature endowed the women of Alcampel, who bear male children, as the carriers of liberty's torch.

Adjacent to the town there is a cemetery called Santa Margarita. In accordance with civil law in 1880, the old woman, Maria del Sabone, asked her family to give her a civil burial when she died. The church was omnipotent at that time and the priest was the lord and master of the village.

The Municipality could not establish a civil cemetery, although it had the right to do so. A short time before the old lady died, a group of young people organised a free-thinker group in Alcampel, among whom was Manuel Blanco, who gave me my ways of thinking. This group saw the priest's pressure against the family and offered their moral and material support to the family. The priest threatened them if they would not allow the church to perform the burial. The freethinker group put pressure on Town Hall and organised a demonstration of all their supporters, demanding compliance with the new law. To avoid trouble the Mayor and the Aldermen made a small enclosure for one grave outside the cemetery wall where the valiant old lady was buried.

The dead must be buried within 24 hours in Spain. This cemetery is known as the 'Corralet de Santa Margarita.' At that time civil burials were rare in Spain.

Little by little the freethinker group embraced a good part of the population. A new cemetery was created in 1888, and the priest and the group confronted each other again.

The priest proposed only 40 square meters for the civil cemetery at the wall opposite the main gate. The struggle was a difficult one. The bishop of Lérida inter-vened personally. (Alcampel belongs to the Lérida diocese). The freethinkers, supported by the liberal population, gained 25% of the area of the enclosed cemetery from the Municipal Council, with the entrance through the main gate and a corridor to the right leading to the civil area.

Since then there have been many non-religious burials during the past century, and many children were not baptised. I remember the civil funerals in my lifetime, some with music – the funeral march, and on the way back the 'Marseillaise' (considered revolutionary). The funeral procession would cross the large plaza in front of the church, even though the priest opposed it.

The church owned estates that were worked by the peasants of Alcampel, who paid the priest one third of the harvest. He would catch the tenant farmers and threaten to throw them off the land if they did not make contributions to the church. They answered that he could put the land out to pasture. However, the statue of Christ was not taken out that year on Holy Thursday because six strong men were needed to carry the figure and they could not be found to do this for the church. The peasants did not leave the land, but the saints were not carried for the church ceremonial. General Francisco Coll Zanuy, from military headquarters and a son of Alcampel, was there that day. When the procession returned to the Church, the general said in a loud voice: 'What kind of a priest are you to allow your parish to escape?' The priest did not breathe a word in reply.

In 1917, a niece of the old freethinker José Fumas (unbaptised) wanted to marry Jaime Gracía of Albelda in a civil ceremony. They filed the necessary papers in both villages, but the two priests and the judge acted in concert to delay the processing of the documents, and they finally got married in the Church. But this trickery kicked back because the uncle, after waiting patiently for a good Sunday, issued a proclamation for a meeting at 4 o'clock in the afternoon in the highway plaza, without announcing the purpose. At 4 p.m. the plaza was full. The balcony of a house opened and Uncle Fumas appeared with the two sweethearts, one on each side of the balcony. The free-thinker spoke of the complicity of the two priests and the judge who did not give them the documents needed for a civil wedding. They were forced to get married in the church. In a loud voice he proclaimed from the balcony: 'It is a crime to prevent these young people from having a civil wedding. Where is the law of justice?' He waved them to approach each other face to face and he asked them in a loud voice: 'Young people, do you love each other?' They answered, 'Yes.' 'Then embrace in the presence of the people.' They did so amid an outburst of applause. When there was silence again, he spoke to the gathering: 'People of Alcampel, you are the witness to this union.' Then two citizens spoke attacking the system of justice and the Church. The second speaker, Manuel Arne, a Storekeeper, spoke of the fabulous myths of the Church that lull the minds and aspirations of the listeners to sleep and he was warmly applauded.

As they were leaving the Plaza two Civil Guards arrived. They took the speakers to the Town Hall and then to Tamarite. Now there was a revolt. A large crowd followed the arrested men, shouting demands for their liberty. The situation looked bad. The judge recognised the danger. He released the prisoners and everyone returned to the village. A few days later a civil wedding took place in Alcampel. These were historic weddings!

Another concern of the village was the education of the children. During the last decade of the past century a large part of the population wanted to get their children out of the State school that drilled their minds with sacred doctrine and history.

Through the efforts of the freethinker group the first independent teacher was brought to the village in 1891, Mr. Brualla. He did good work in every respect until 1895. It was not easy at that time to find a liberal teacher for a small community like Alcampel, as compared with the large cities.

In 1905, another private school was established with don Ángel Durán as the teacher. This was the first school that I attended together with my brother, who was four years older than me. Its existence was precarious and it lasted barely two years. But our dreams were realised early in 1909. Not just a teacher came this time, but don Manuel Nuñez, a rationalist teacher, and he opened a rationalist school that lasted until 1919. From the beginning the student registration was not full. It cost two pesetas plus the cost of books and materials. It was difficult to pay, but parents overcame every difficulty. Don Manuel was a friend of the pedagogue Francisco Ferrer y Guardia, founder of the Modern School, who was shot by the reaction in the ditches of Montjuich in Barcelona, October 13 1909.

When children reached the age of 12 to 14 years, most families had to send them out to work. Those of us who had the good fortune to study with don Manuel know how to write a letter and we know some arithmetic. We young people grew up free of prejudice and servility to God, King and master. How often do I think of don Manuel! We had another liberal school from 1921 to 1924, and still another liberal school in 1931 with Sr. Giménez as the teacher. On January 1 1932, a comrade, a member of the Teachers and Liberal Professions Union of Barcelona, and a son of Alcampel (whose name I refrain from mentioning out of modesty) made all his knowledge available to the children. He used the teaching methods of the Modern School, which were adopted throughout Spain in schools that were conducted by CNT teachers. Unfortunately, the school was open only two years. It was closed down December 9, 1933, when the teacher was arrested for taking part in the revolutionary uprising.

What liberal roots, spirit and educational effort in Alcampel! It was all done with a lack of material means and with quite a number of illiterate parents who loved and nourished the seeds of liberty. The seeds of the Freethinker Group and the teachers of the New School bore good fruit in Alcampel.

In November 1911, while I was still a child, I remember a heated debate between a young man, Tomás Grau, 30 years of age, and a 60-year-old man after Manuel Pardiñas assassinated José Canalejas, President of the Council of Ministers. The young man spoke of anarchism and collectives. He quoted Bakunin, Malatesta, Anselmo Lorenzo, etc., and he never went to the cafés. Another spokesman for anarchism in Alcampel was Ramón Brualla who in 1918, at the age of 22, was on the Strike Committee of La Canadiense, a large company that was building the Camaras Dam in Lerida Province. Years later his three younger brothers joined the CNT, introduced to anarchism by their brother.

In 1921, a number of young people organised the first labour union in Alcampel affiliated with the CNT. It was closed down and reopened several times until Primo de Rivera closed it down completely on September 13, 1923. I was away from Alcampel from 1919 until the end of 1931.

When the Republic was established in 1931, a CNT Labour Union was organised with many serious, dynamic young people who understood the ideals, and they did not smoke or drink alcohol. They maintained a large library where they were to be found every evening, and they conducted discussions. An art group was formed in which Pilar Gómez and Pilar Ardanuy participated. Social theatrical works were presented in the village and neighbouring communities which created a formidable environment (Examples: 'El Sol de la Humanidad' – Sun of Humanity, 'Los Malos Pastores' The Bad Shepherds, 'El Pan de Piedra' – Bread of Stone, 'El Senor Feudal' – The Feudal Lord, etc.).

People did not work as employees of others in the village. It was the young, small farmers, of good homes, who joined the CNT. They opposed politics and its hangers-on, and supported the CNT-FAI position and abstention in the elections. Among them were the brothers Trenc, Sopena, Arcau, Blanco, Pomac, Sallan, Buira, Nadal, etc. Shortly before the November 1933 elections, a delegation of the Radical Socialist Party held a campaign meeting at a large cafe. The place was filled. Some of the comrades sat close to the speakers.

The first speaker said, 'We have a number of good projects prepared for the Republic. (They wanted to calm the workers down because of past wounds.) We want to improve life, stabilise individual and collective liberty.' On hearing the word liberty we cannot keep silent. We ask if we can speak after they have finished or whether we can interrupt while they are speaking. After some hesitation they answered that we could have the floor after they finish. The second speaker spoke in the same way: liberty, justice and a thousand promises. When we were given the floor, the comrade who had interrupted the first speaker pointed out that they had not kept the promises of the Republic incorporated in the Pact of San Sebastian, or in the press conferences during the campaigns of April 12 and June 28 1931.

'You do not fulfil the demands of the workers. The politicians of the left make concessions, but only to the reactionaries. Where has the Agrarian Reform been carried out? Why has the Republic not dissolved the Civil Guard that the people demanded so strongly? On the contrary, the Assault Guard was created to the sorrow of the CNT.

'On April 18th the 'Law Against Vagrants' was passed, followed by the 'Fugitive Law'. Can you cite a single case when these laws were used against a capitalist? No. They have been used only against workers, and in particular, against members of the CNT.

'When the first orator spoke of liberty, I was indignant and I could not remain silent. How is it possible for representatives of the Radical Socialist Party to be so cynical as to speak of liberty when the Minister of Justice, Botella Asensio, a member of your party, has imprisoned 40,000 members of the CNT for no other crime than defending the interests of the workers? After your Minister opens the doors of Spain's prisons, when the deportees to Bata on the ship *Buenos Aires* have been allowed to return, then you can speak of liberty, but not until then.'

He finished his remarks with the following words to the audience: 'You, the exploited, must judge!' There was an outburst of applause. The party speakers did not offer a word in their own defence and left on the run. The Radical

Socialist Party could not find supporters for their campaign or to serve as tellers at the voting; 42% of the village abstained in the voting.

According to plans worked out, and the meeting at Monumental Plaza in Barcelona, the revolution was to start December 8 1933, at midnight. If the train from Saragossa did not pass it meant that the movement had started there. That was the signal.

We started the movement after establishing contact with the Region and the comrades at Alguaire. Joaquín Ardanuy gave us the key to the barn where relief groups were waiting. It was raining. There were two control groups on the highway, at the entrance and exit of the village. When we heard the whistle of the Saragossa train, we realised that we had been mistaken but we could not, we dared not retreat.

A man from Barcelona had retired to live in Alcampel with a youth from the village. He was 55 years old, strong, agile, brutal and a supporter of reaction. He knew how to handle arms well and was very dangerous. We had the difficult assignment to seize and disarm him. We were told he was at the cinema. The northern control group was to ambush him. As he returned to his house he saw us 60 meters away. Without a moment's hesitation he opened fire with a gun in each hand. He fired first and killed the comrade Nogueros. We returned the shots and disappeared into the night. On the ninth of December, at 5 o'clock in the morning, we burned the Town Hall records and files (not the library or the furniture), and proclaimed libertarian communism. We examined the records and saw the injustice and inequality of taxes for the rich and the poor. Suddenly, we saw the man who had killed Noguero and we chased after him. He ran into a house and jumped into a pigsty to defend himself. We called upon him to throw away his weapons and nothing would happen to him. His reply as always was to fire at us with a gun in each hand. We set the pigsty on fire with gasoline. How brave he was! He preferred to die in the fire rather than surrender.

We placed a red and black banner on the Town Hall and proclaimed libertarian communism. Comrade Sopena made a detailed statement of our goals in the new libertarian society, namely the abolition of private property and with it money. The stores were to be prepared to give the people necessary food with vouchers that would be redeemed by the Revolutionary Committee. Abuses of any type would be checked severely, without hesitation. A new moral order must be established.

When the passenger bus arrived from Graus and Benabarre at half-past-nine, a delegation was waiting at Jaime Noguero's restaurant where the bus stops. Written notification was given the driver that the Committee was requisitioning the bus, a similar method to that used with the innkeeper to provide lodgings to travellers. Vouchers would be exchanged for provisions by the stores.

We learned from the Regional and District Committees that the railroad workers had declared a general strike. There was a total blackout of news during the morning of the ninth. We did not know if the movement had spread. The silence caused certain uneasiness. It had rained all night but the morning was clear and bright.

The plain ends 3 kilometres southeast of the village. At that point there is a declining slope, more or less steep mountains that dominate the vast 'La Litera' prairie. When the weather is clear and a breeze comes from the south it is possible to hear the train whistle. What a disappointment! There could be no doubt. The railroads had not declared a strike, or if they had, it was crushed.

Absolute silence was maintained about the situation. In spite of the disappointments demoralisation could not be allowed to set in. Our cards had been played. We could not, we must not turn back. We knew how to accept the consequences. During the week we took care of two priests, accompanying them to the Marcelo Cafe where they ate and slept. They were assured no harm would be done them, but if they tried to escape they would have to take the consequences. During the two days that we lived in libertarian communism they did not conduct any religious service. Entrance and exit from the village remained controlled, but no one was travelling. There were no strangers. Even the Civil Guard from Tamarite and Albelda did not dignify us with a visit. Were they under orders not to move? Certainly.

On the morning of the tenth, Doctor Argo – who was a fascist, was told to look at the two victims of the day before who had been brought to the cemetery. He was asked to extend the period for burial, which he did without raising any objections. After the forms were filled, the two bodies were buried.

The same morning a rumour circulated – without being able to trace its origin – that a column of Civil Guards was coming from Graus to crush our movement. On their own initiative a number of comrades went to the Inn and ordered the bus driver to drive to the Saganta Bridge, about 15 kilometres north of the village. They drilled several holes at the base of the centre pillar (the bridge had three arches 10 to 15 meters high). They placed sticks of dynamite with which they would strike a good blow. They wanted to postpone the expected arrival of the Civil Guards, hoping to receive word of a general uprising for which we were still waiting. Unfortunately, no word came. I do not think it necessary to point out that the insurrectionary movement was not supported by the whole organisation.

On the afternoon of the tenth, a company of machine gunners arrived from Huesca, as well as a contingent of 80 Civil Guards under the command of an officer. At a distance of one kilometre from the village the armed forces took up positions on two sides: the machine gunners took positions on the dominating hills to the southwest; the Civil Guards on the southeast entered the village little by little without encountering any resistance. What kind of resistance could be offered by people armed with only a few pistols and hunting rifles against machine guns and well armed Civil Guards? Young comrade Pomar was the only one to resist. He fired a few cartridges against them as they came up the Street of Fountains. After an exchange of shots from which he fortunately escaped unharmed, he threw away his gun and ran away looking for refuge. During the night he reached Camporréls, a village 18 kilometres northeast from Alcampel.

It seems that the Civil Guards had orders not to give Pomar the customary order 'Halt!' but to shoot him on sight. Pomar had to change his hiding place frequently because of the sophisticated means available to the Civil Guards for hunting down a refugee. Toward the end of December he was hiding in a house in the centre of Tamarite and decided to surrender to the court. Surely his life would be saved by this step.

After the village was recaptured, the red and black banner was taken down and replaced by the republican flag. The 'conquering' force patrolled the streets all night.

On the morning of the eleventh they started to arrest members of the CNT. We had the honour to be the first, followed by many members and sympathisers of the Agricultural Union, and political opponents of local reaction. Our correct attitude and conduct gained the sympathy and admiration of the majority in the community for us. The second floor of the Town Hall was used as a temporary prison. Little by little all who were involved in the Movement were brought in, as well as some who had nothing to do with the insurrection, but were victims of hatred of right-wingers.

A special judge was named and he began to take statements. The author of this report made his statement. Three days later I was turned over to the Civil Governor of the Province as a prisoner of the government. I expected to be set free sooner or later. The arrests mounted. We were sixty or seventy, or more. On the morning of the 15th they called out ten of the prisoners and I was among them. We were the first group to leave. We were not able to speak to our wives. They put us into a van accompanied by eight guards. We did not know where we were going. When we reached Binéfar we noted that the van took the road to Monzón. We were taken to Huesca, to be placed in the old barracks of San Vicente. There were a large number of prisoners including a number from Albarate de Cinca. Among them was Carrasquer, a highly cultured man and father of sons very well known in the CNT. The atmosphere was excellent and morale very high. We were all there for having fought in the same cause. Because more and more prisoners were arriving daily, the prison director organised a special train of about 400 prisoners to be taken elsewhere. We were bound together by the wrists in rows of five and taken to the Estudios Barracks at Jaca. Three years earlier, December 13, 1930, Captains Galán, García Hernández and Salinas had issued the proclamation of the Republic at the Jaca Barracks.

I must speak of the great sympathy of the workers in Jaca for us. The day we arrived they took up a collection and bought tobacco, biscuits, etc. which they brought to the director of the prison for distribution to us. New expeditions of prisoners arrived daily. When they entered the barracks courtyard we sang '*Hijos del Pueblo*' ('Sons of the People,' the song of the CNT-FAI) and cheered for the Social Revolution. Finally the prison director arranged to receive the prisoners in the street because we on the inside raised a tremendous clamour and cursing against the uniformed guards, and tempers ran high. There were more than 40,000 CNT prisoners during the month of November, more than all the common prisoners in jail. The addition of all those arrested in the December Movement raised the prison population enormously. They did not know where to place the swollen population.

They continued to arrest people in the village, sending them in batches to Tamarite. As they were indicted they were sent to Huesca with the majority going to Jaca. Six members of my family were arrested, including my sister Maria. Young Pomar was in one of the groups of prisoners. He was the one who tried to fight the Civil Guards as they entered the village. One of the Civil

Guards asked him ironically: 'Pomar, what would you have done if your Movement had triumphed?'

'Sir guard,' he responded with equal irony, 'Nothing. Absolutely nothing. The only thing we would have done is raise your pay!'

'You rascal,' the guard replied. 'Sure! You would have raised our pay!'

The indicted, perhaps 50 (I do not remember exactly), including the two women who took the gasoline to pour on the pigsty, were taken to Jaca (except for those who remained in Huesca) for their trials. The lawyer, Vilarroda, an excellent defence attorney for jailed CNT members, took on the defence of almost all the prisoners. Some were released, including a neighbour of Maria Blanco. Maria was condemned in advance. The parish priest used his influence to release the first and condemn the second in spite of the brilliant defence of the lawyer who asked for clemency and freedom for his client, mother of four sons. She hoped that justice would not be so cruel as to deprive four innocent children of the love and care of their mother. The public prosecutor asked for 10 years in prison, which was finally reduced to three years and one day. We were most indignant. Maria Blanco had not been baptised. She had had a civil marriage in 1915. None of her four sons has been baptised. The clergy could not pardon such 'heresy.' She was placed in prison at Jaca to serve her sentence. The remainder of the condemned — I do not remember how many, perhaps 30 were taken to prison at Chinchilla (Albacete) for their sentences. Those who attacked the regime were given ten-year sentences and those who tried to destroy the Saganta Bridge were given twenty-four year sentences. While we were in jail at Jaca the majority of the people gave us their moral and material support.

In spite of the repression of the right-wing government, which differed very little from the left-wing government as far as the CNT was concerned, the agitation, strikes, sabotage continued. Voices rose everywhere demanding amnesty for the prisoners. Finally the government had to yield to the pressure of the people and grant a partial amnesty. In the first days of May 1934, my brother and sister, Maria and Manolo, returned to the village, as well as the other comrades from Chinchilla who were condemned to ten years imprisonment. Those who were condemned to twenty-four years imprisonment were reduced to fourteen years and they remained in jail until April 1936, when total amnesty was declared for all political and social prisoners. When the last prisoners were returned from Chinchilla to liberal and libertarian Alcampel they were given a tremendous reception. Thus ended the revolutionary epic of December 8th, 1933.

I have related some of the liberal characteristics of the village and the continuing history will confirm it further.

While I was still a child I remember hearing the rich people in Alcampel express the wish to have a Civil Guard post in the village, but it always met with such strong opposition that they could not achieve their aim. The attempt at revolution gave them their opportunity. When order was completely restored a corporal and four soldiers remained in the village. The bourgeois families competed with each other to offer them shelter in their homes. When the panic had passed, they were happy to rub elbows with 'civilians.' At the beginning they took turns having a soldier in their house. Finally, all five soldiers who made up the military establishment stayed with the merchant José Amoros. The reaction had a free hand to do what they had wanted to do all along and they used this opportunity to achieve their goal of building a small barracks. They had their long desired Civil Guard, but they did not have suitable housing for them. With the anarcho-syndicalists in prison and the rest of the population intimidated, they felt they were masters of the world.

There is a small hill in the southeast section of the village that dominates the community. That was the location selected for the barracks. The opposition councilmen continued to oppose the project on the ground that the municipality would have to pay the full cost. The project moved ahead in spite of the opposition. When the treasurer did not have the 100,000 pesetas that the builder asked for, several of the large landholders and political bosses mortgaged some properties with a bank in Barbastro to obtain the loan. They expected that in time the village would pay the cost. The barracks was discussed everywhere, the supporters praising it, those in the opposition disagreeing. They spoke of having a room for 'beatings'. They used every means possible to achieve their aim but they did not succeed.

They scheduled a plebiscite for a Sunday early in June. This is when the majority of the people are working at the harvest in the Litera plain. They expected that the people would not lose a precious day of harvesting just to vote. They were wrong. Participation in the vote was complete and 63% voted NO to the barracks. The work was not stopped entirely. It continued to go ahead slowly. I will explain later who started the barracks.

July 19 and Alcampel

As was to be expected, the elections of February 1936 returned the Left to power. This upset the reactionaries very seriously. They were not satisfied with the concessions the government made to them. They tried to obstruct the work of the new government and they wanted particularly to destroy the CNT, their greatest enemy. It was no secret that the fascists were preparing to overthrow the government. The only ones who pretended to be ignorant were the members of the government. They continued to offer the fascists every facility to go on with their project. Everyone knew that appointing Franco military head of the Canary Islands would give him the freedom to organise the movement and establish contact with leading fascist elements outside Spain. On the mainland they had to act carefully, but on the islands they could make their moves in the open. The attitude of the Left government toward the CNT did not change. Social conflicts continued, as did the arrest of workers. Nothing like that happened when the 'Legionnaires' of Doctor Albiñana had demonstrations. If at times one of these were arrested for the sake of appearances, he entered the police station through one door and walked out through another.

Since they had the support of the majority of the people, why did not the Government use the laws it had on the books to maintain 'public order' against the 'Legionnaires' and their leader? Because the sons of the Pope and the real villains must not be disturbed. Capitalism was afraid of social revolution. The leaders of the Republican Parties and the Socialist Party, including Indalecio Prieto, shared this fear. They wanted to serve the organization, to share power, but not move against the interests of the privileged classes. They followed our Movement closely and were fully informed about our programs including that adopted by the Congress of Saragossa, which opened May 1, 1936. Our goal was the establishment of libertarian communism in Spain. This was no secret for anyone. Everyone was waiting for the fascists to launch their attack and we of the CNT maintained a constant vigil.

The Movement of 1936

I remember July 18. After supper my neighbours and I went out to the street for some fresh air. At about 11 o'clock that night a rumour reached us that the army had risen against the Republic in Morocco. There were only five radios in the village: one at the Agricultural Union, another at the Café Mancelo generally patronised by people without clearly defined opinions, another at Doctor Arjo's office, and the others in private homes. The following day, the 19th, CNT members gathered at the Union's cafe and exchanged information and impressions as we followed the news on the radio. At 10 o'clock, Radio Barcelona announced that the army had risen yesterday (Saturday) in Morocco and that the head of the Government, Santiago Casares Quiroga, speaking on Radio Madrid that night, said: 'It seems that the fascists have risen in Madrid. If they have risen, I am going to bed.'

Did you ever see greater cynicism? At one o'clock Radio Barcelona confirmed the news and gave details of the resistance of the workers in the Protectorate and the rest of Spain, especially the workers in Barcelona. They had come out in force against the rebels. The general uprising was a fact. There was no doubt now.

The Civil Guard must have received orders to remain

in the barracks because, contrary to custom, no uniform was to be seen in the streets. There was uneasiness in every face. Somebody had to organise, take the initiative. The CNT members met at the headquarters of the Agricultural Union with the Left Republicans who had the majority of members in the Union. Our arsenal consisted of some pistols and a few hunting shotguns. In view of the gravity of the situation, the creation of a Revolutionary Committee was suggested with four members, two from each organisation. The majority of the Left Republicans present were uncertain about joining the Committee, but we pointed out that if fascism triumphed there was no future for us and they would share the same fate. They finally accepted the proposal and a Revolutionary Committee was created. The local fascists came out to the streets during the night without noticing that the Civil Guards were not there with them. They probably felt that they were masters of the situation and that the Guards would come to their aid if necessary. Our lights went out at midnight. Someone had broken the transformer and the town was in darkness. The situation did not look good. The Committee that was now organised ordered guards at the entrance to the building and on the balconies. We did not think that they would attack the building, but under the circumstances it was prudent to take all necessary precautions. The watch ended at two o'clock in the morning and nothing had happened. Everyone went home in the morning, with a member of the Committee on duty at all times guarded by armed antifascists. The area was filled with news and rumours.

On the morning of the twentieth, the Lieutenant of the Civil Guards at Tamarite ordered the officers of the six posts in the town to concentrate all forces in Tamarite, including sergeants, corporals and guards. Barcelona was almost completely in our hands, but Madrid and other places were still in revolt. The majority in our town were with the CNT. At the Union café Pedro Nan of the Agricultural Union, who changed his colours easily, asked me to take a walk with him. I accepted.

He said: 'Victor, what do you think of this Movement?'

'What do you think?' I replied.

He answered: 'You are intelligent, Victor. I therefore feel that I can suggest to you that we keep things quiet here so that nothing will happen to either side.' The reactionaries had sent him.

I listened, and when he finished I pushed back his outstretched hand and said: 'I speak only for myself (not for the CNT). I am not surprised that you are doing this. I tell you and whoever sent you: I know who my enemies were, who they are today and who they will be tomorrow, whatever happens.'

On the twenty-first we knew that the reactionaries were armed and that we had to disarm them. An edict was published which stated: 'The Revolutionary Committee calls upon all citizens who have weapons to turn them over to the Committee by 2 P.M. Those who refuse will be taken by force.'

Alcampel, July 21 1936.

Not one gun was turned in.

We controlled the entrance and exit of the town. No one could leave without a pass. When the Civil Guard left the fascists were demoralised.

There was an opening in the wall of the vestry

behind a bookcase that led to the patio of the Civil Guard residence giving the Civil Guards and fascists access to the Tower.

The priest disappeared on the 19th. When we searched through his papers and records in his house we saw photographs of married women and young girls. What were these photos doing here, especially the married women? There could be no doubt. How far these people went!

On the 27th, with the threat from Tamarite gone, the members of the CNT decided to start carrying out our aims, to try to create something new and humane, to organise an agricultural collective in accordance with anarchist principles. We held a meeting to determine how the idea should be presented to the people. We had the sympathy of the people but we knew we had to act carefully when we dealt with the personal interests of individuals. We agreed to call a public assembly of the area through the Alcampel Labour Union at 9 o'clock in the evening in the Plaza Mayor.

The call could not be made in the name of the Revolutionary Committee, which included two members of the Left Republicans who belonged to the Agricultural Union. They had agreed to join the Revolutionary Committee because they were threatened by the same danger as we: we were all antifascists. But they were not collectivists. They tried to boycott our efforts. However, they failed because of the influence of our organisation with the peasants.

At the appointed hour the Plaza was filled with people. Comrade Joaquín Sopena spoke from the balcony of the cafe owned by the fascist Leoncio Carrera (where the collective was organised). He spoke at length explaining the goals of fascism, which wants to turn back the clock in Spain several centuries and suppress all collective and individual liberty. The uprising that they started and the resistance of the workers provide the opportunity to realise our dream of liberty and justice. We idealists must make the Social Revolution while we fight the war. We must end the exploitation of man by man, transform loafers and idlers into productive workers, and create a new society together where all will be producers and consumers.

In accordance with our method of procedure a Chairman and Secretaries were elected. I was chosen to be Chairman of this historic assembly and Comrades Sopena and Trenc were named Secretaries. We went to the centre of the balcony. I opened the meeting, adding to Comrade Sopena's remarks. I explained the goals we had in mind, an Agricultural Collective where all would have the same obligations and the same rights and benefits. The new organization that we proposed to create would be completely free, libertarian. No one would be compelled – no one could be compelled – to join the new organization. Compulsion would be starting on a false foundation, a denial of our principles. Those who wish to join do so freely. The collectivists will bring what they possess to the organization. The concept 'yours and mine' will no longer exist when the Collective is established. Everything will belong to everyone. An Administrative Council will be elected by a majority vote for one year at a General Assembly. If any questionable actions are observed during the year, the Assembly will be sovereign, will be able to withdraw its vote of confidence and require the administrators to resign.

The Collective will not use money internally. All members of the Administrative Council – except for the General Secretary – will be required to work when they have free time from their administrative responsibilities. Work groups of ten comrades will be organised, with one elected as group delegate. He will be in touch with the Council to organise the work because the properties of the CNT comrades are scattered throughout the village. There will be no more servants or housemaids throughout the area. The exploitation of man is abolished.

After I finished we made it clear that what we want to do is not the idea, or program, of one man or one group. Everyone is invited to offer their suggestions and opinions. Ask questions and everyone may judge whether the answers are adequate. We know that the lone individual is a small entity. Together we are everything. Help us! Give us your support and collaboration and we will create everything together! Fascism is definitely defeated. A new society is on the march. No one's liberty will be restrained in the CNT. I therefore ask everyone at this great and historic assembly to speak freely on the proposed Collective. Light will come out of the discussion and reasoning.

A number of people asked for the floor and the Secretary took their names in order. The first speaker was Dr. Antonio Pujol, the doctor for the Agricultural Union, a member of the POUM (Trotskyist Party). He started by saying that we were not offering anything new by starting a Collective because there is one already in the Agricultural Union where the members go to the bakery in the union for their bread. He then went on to political questions. He was also unconvincing when he stated that the remarks of the first speaker and the Chairman of the Assembly only created confusion in the audience.

I replied stating that I knew all about the operations and goals of the Agricultural Union. It was started by large- and medium-sized property holders and includes a number of less fortunate peasants with small pieces of inferior land at the north end of the Municipality. The first and second groups bring their wheat to the Union warehouse during the month of September. This assures them enough bread for the entire year. As for the almost disinherited, they have used up their reserves by December or January in the majority of cases. They must buy bread on credit and pay for it as they can. It is true that the members of all three categories take their coffee together in the union cafe. Some of the day labourers who were exploited all week sit together with their bosses on Sunday and play cards. It is also true that the boss' wife can prepare a meal with all the necessary nutrition for her children while the day labourer does so with great difficulty. I suppose that Dr. Pujol has observed the great difference in the standard of living of the two classes of citizens when he visits the homes of the sick who are rich and those who are practically disinherited.

We ask that exploitation be ended forever. Let everyone work according to his ability and consume according to his needs. Work for all, bread also for all. This is the foundation principle of the Collective that we members of the CNT propose and which we want to encompass all of society – an end to capitalism and money.

A number of people took the floor to seek clarification of various questions. One member of the audience asked: 'If you are thinking of abolishing money, how will you be able to make purchases?'

In the CNT at the national level there are Federations of Industry. The land that we work will produce cereals, vegetables, fruits, fodder and cattle more than we need for our own consumption. We will have a surplus that we will deposit with a District or Regional Depository in a central area. The Industry Federations will deposit their surplus manufactured goods. At this point there will be an interchange of goods. Each of the Collectives will have an open account with the District Depository that will record the value of our deposited merchandise and the value of the manufactured goods we receive. A general balance will be drawn up semi-annually so that each Collective will know its economic condition.

Another question dealt with the distribution of food. I answered this very interesting question as follows: all cereals, fruits, vegetables, everything produced on the land will be brought to the Collective Depository where part will be set aside for consumption by the members of the Collective, part will be reserved for seed, and part will be grain for the livestock. The balance will be brought to the District Depository. A Consumers' Cooperative will be organised where the women will go daily for their provisions, which will be issued according to the size of the family. In other words, no one will be hungry, or without the food needed to sustain life. I went on to explain how transportation would be organised, and the trades, housing, culture and propaganda, etc. Finally, it seemed to me that everything had been said that could orient and influence the audience.

When the agenda was completed I stated: All citizens who, with full responsibility for their action, wish to join the new organization can do so freely today, tomorrow or when they wish. The doors will be open to all who wish to join. The Administrative Council will be elected by majority vote at the first General Assembly. All members will participate in drawing up the rules and regulations under which the Collective will function. Although we members of the CNT have an outline of what can be done, the collaboration of all members is essential.

There being no further statements or suggestions I adjourned the 'historic assembly.'

That night and for the next two or three nights a large number of neighbours signed up. Two hundred and fifty families joined the Collective, about half the population of the Municipality. A number of large property owners signed up when they saw that they would have no more servants and day labourers. They were afraid (although they were treated with full respect) that they had no recourse except to join. A number of artisans joined the Collective, including three masons, a jeweller, a blacksmith, a barber, a dressmaker, Teresina, who was Trenc's comrade, etc. A few days later, the doctor of the Agricultural Union who had challenged our new system of living at the Assembly made an application to join the Collective, which gave us satisfaction.

The Collective started to function on the 29th, but there were an infinity of problems to take care of, among them transportation. We did not have a truck. There were three citizens in the area who had trucks and earned their living with their trucks. But none of them joined the Collective because they were afraid to give up their only means of earning a livelihood. How shall we get a truck? Someone suggested that perhaps we could arrange for an exchange with a company. When one is young decisions are made quickly, and particularly then. We decided to contact the three largest of the four companies in the area. We took a truck and went to the Ford Company in Barcelona with comrades Trenc and Pomar. The Ford Company had been socialised. We asked for Comrade Vallejo, whom we knew, an outstanding CNT member, and he received us warmly. We explained the purpose of our visit: to see if it would be possible to make an exchange. We brought three church bells to exchange for a 1929 truck that was still in running condition. After overcoming various objections, they agreed to give us a new truck in exchange for the bells. There was great joy in Alcampel when we returned with the problem solved so quickly.

The Collective Begins to Function

Production of wheat, corn, beetroot and alfalfa: work groups are organised with a delegate for each group. All the delegates meet each evening to organise the work. The first thing we did was to harvest the wheat that was being damaged by the drought.

There were two threshing machines and we requisitioned one of them. In addition to one tractor we had six pairs of mules for the farm. We requisitioned the 'Roque' farm, irrigated land belonging to the Marques of Alfarràs, where we cultivated sufficient vegetables to feed 250 families.

We carried on a number of experiments in a corner of the irrigated land where we cultivated castor oil and seedbeds for the vegetable garden.

Many comrades turned over their land to the

Collective.

There were groups who worked outside the village all week and came home Saturdays. Their delegate met with the other delegates to plan the work. We had two farms, one for poultry and the other for hogs. In addition to enough meat for our own consumption, we were able to issue 25 kilograms of pork to each adult and a little less to each child. The surplus was brought to the District Depository at Binéfar.

Two companies were requisitioned, a textile mill and an export house. Local business was not touched. We organised a dressmaking shop, a barbershop and a butcher shop.

We had our own local money. However, we also had a Collective Treasury when we had to use regular currency for replacements from the outside, operations for the sick and medications for the pharmacy, all of which was paid for by the Committee.

A dining room was set up to feed patrols passing through, as well as the elderly.

Pilar Ardanuy washed their clothing and delivered it. How happy the old people were who lived alone! No previous regime had ever had the slightest concern for their welfare. We prohibited the sale of alcohol in the cafés. Theatrical works were presented in the church.

There was a large, very fertile field in the northern part of the town, more than 100 hectares, called 'La Cuadra.' Each family fixed the boundaries of their property with landmarks. These landmarks were removed and the field became one parcel of land. The land was cultivated with a tractor and it was a marvel to behold. What joy to see the transformation! From slave labour to a chance to rest, from misery to abundance.

All wars bring destruction of people and property, but not ours.

Catalonia sent gardening experts to organise the Collectives and teach them how to keep the towns free. Among them was José Viadiu, whom I knew personally in *Solidaridad Obrera* ('Worker Solidarity', the CNT daily newspaper in Barcelona, which had the largest circulation in the city during the Civil War). He wrote a good report on the progress of our Collective.

While attending a meeting in Graus, I went to see the statue of Joaquín Costa, a liberal, progressive man, and a Deputy. Among his various books he wrote *Agrarian Collective*, a very good book. He was a journalist and collaborator on *Solidaridad Obrera*. He was arrested in Saragossa and died in 1911 in Graus.

At the end of August, Puig Elias of CENU (CNT Teachers Union) called and asked me to work with him. A column of children had arrived the Aragón front and he wanted to take care of them. I accepted. Three comrades went to Barcelona. We did not think that that would be the last time we would see Alcampel. We were unable to return because of the advance of the fascist troops.

The members of the Collective reached the Pyrenees and passed over the border to France.

Victor Blanco

About Victor Blanco

This impassioned report by Augustin Souchy, direct observer of the collectives in Aragón, has the subtitle '*Libertarian Communism in the Liberated Areas*'. It is a reproduction of the Tierra y Libertad (Land and Liberty) Edition, Barcelona, 1937. We took the liberty in this new edition to add an appendix not included in Souchy's original book. It casts light on some of the small and great daily struggles experienced by the Aragón collectives.

A veteran fighter from Alacampel, Victor Blanco, a refugee from 1939 until his death in 1976, compiled his written recollections of his town, Alcampel, and the struggles of its peasants.

Victor Blanco was born in Alcampel at the end of the last century. His father, Joaquin Blanco, was a small farmer. During the First Republic he belonged to the anti-clerical and anti-monarchical groups called 'gabarrons' (after the principle founder, the ex-priest Bartolome Gabarro) who advocated secular education.

At 15 years of age, Victor went to Barcelona to look for work. He came to know the revolutionary experience of Francisco Ferrer y Guardia, the Modern School. He obtained a licence to teach. The Agricultural Union of Alcampel asked him to return home and teach. He returned to his village and married Julia Ardanuy. He conducted classes from 1930 to 1935, teaching children of both sexes to age 14 during the day, and in the winter teaching adults in the evening. He was a rationalist teacher, a friend of the children. He did not use rewards or punishment. 1936 comes, and the collectives. But Puig Elias, head of the CNT Teachers Union, asks him to work in CENU. Then 1939, exile and death far from his own land.

The text comes to our attention when two comrades of Victor Blanco wanted to transcribe the original text. One dictated and the other typed. There were many typographical and grammatical errors in the text. We edited out the errors which would have made it difficult to understand, and retained his style. We did a minimum of editing in order to retain the original text of a rationalist teacher. A humane testimonial that tells us much more about the libertarian struggles of our recent past than any erudite or 'scientific' study.